Irish Women Writers: Texts and Contexts

Series editors: **Kathryn Laing and Sinéad Mooney**

Elke d'Hoker (ed.), *Ethel Colburn Mayne: Selected Stories*
Kathryn Laing (ed.), *Hannah Lynch's Irish Girl Rebels: 'A Girl Revolutionist' and 'Marjory Maurice'*
James H. Murphy (ed.), *Rosa Mulholland, Feminist, Victorian, Catholic and Patriot*

Advisory Board:
Heidi Hansson, Margaret Kelleher, Gerardine Meaney,
James H. Murphy

Advance acclaim

'Rosa Mulholland was one of the most prominent authors of her day, both popular and pioneering. Her work provides perspectives on late nineteenth-century Irish history and politics, but it is also highly relevant for critical studies of, for example, genre development, feminism and eco-criticism. James H. Murphy's excellent introduction and the well-chosen selections will engage new generations of readers and scholars'.

– **Heidi Hansson**, author of *Emily Lawless 1845–1913: Writing the Interspace* and editor of *New Contexts: Re-Framing Nineteenth-Century Women's Prose.*

Rosa Mulholland
Feminist, Victorian, Catholic and Patriot

For David Hayden

IRISH WOMEN WRITERS
Texts and Contexts

ROSA MULHOLLAND: FEMINIST, VICTORIAN, CATHOLIC AND PATRIOT

JAMES H. MURPHY

EER
Edward Everett Root, Publishers, Brighton, 2021.

EER
Edward Everett Root, Publishers, Co. Ltd.,
Atlas Chambers, 33 West Street, Brighton, Sussex, BN1 2RE,
England.
Full details of our overseas agents in America, Australia, Canada, China, Europe, and Japan and how to order our books are given on our website.
www.eerpublishing.com

edwardeverettroot@yahoo.co.uk

© James H. Murphy 2021.

Rosa Mulholland Feminist, Victorian, Catholic and Patriot

ISBN: 9781913087715 Paperback
ISBN: 9781913087722 Hardback
ISBN: 9781913087739 eBook

Irish Women Writers: Texts and Contexts Series, volume 3.

This edition © Edward Everett Root Publishers Co. Ltd., 2021.

James H. Murphy has asserted his right to be identified as the owner of the copyright of this Work in accordance with the Copyright, Designs and Patents Act 1988 as the owner of this Work.

All rights reserved. No part of this publication may be reproduced, stored in a retrieval system or transmitted in any form or by any means, electronic, mechanical, photocopying, recording or otherwise, without the prior permission of the copyright owner.

Design and production by Pageset Ltd., High Wycombe, Buckinghamshire.

Contents

Introduction ix

1. *Dunmara* (Volume Three: Chapters Three and Eleven [extract]) 1

2. 'The Hungry Death' 21

3. *Marcella Grace* (Chapters Eleven to Thirteen) 49

4. 'Wanted an Irish Novelist' 83

5. *Nanno, A Daughter of the State* (Chapters Fifteen to Seventeen) 93

6. *The Return of Mary O'Murrough* (Chapters Ten to Twelve) 117

7. Selected Poems 141

Select Bibliography 151

The editor

JAMES H MURPHY has been Professor of English at DePaul University, Chicago, and at Boston College. He is a scholar of nineteenth-century Ireland. He is the author of six monographs and editor or co-editor of ten works including *The Oxford History of the Irish Book, iv, 1800–1891* (2011). His principal areas of research are the political history and the history of fiction of the century. He has published three monographs over the past decade, *Irish Novelists and the Victorian Age* (Oxford, 2011) *Ireland's Czar: Gladstonian Government and the Lord Lieutenancies of the Red Earl Spencer, 1868–1886* (2014) and *The Politics of Dublin Corporation, 1840–1900: From Reform to Expansion* (2020).

Acknowledgement

The editor is grateful to the Reverend Gregory Kalscheur, SJ, Dean of the Morrissey College of Arts and Sciences at Boston College for financial assistance toward the production of this book.

Introduction

Rosa Mulholland (1841–1921) was one of the most significant and popular Irish women writers of her era.¹ She produced poems, novels, short stories, several short plays, works for children, religious works, essays on travel and on social issues, biography and work as an archival editor. Even today some of her work strikes a decidedly feminist tone, but she combined this with an advocacy for her Catholic faith that may challenge the assumptions of today's readers. This book offers the reader extracts and whole texts that illustrate the more important trends in her writing. They have been chosen on the basis of being significant interventions by Mulholland on various issues and also as being illustrative of the variety of topics she addressed at different points in her career.

Mulholland did not leave an archive of her personal correspondence. Perhaps something might be gained by a trawl through the archives of her contemporaries. What can readily be retrieved about her life comes from an appreciation that Matthew Russell wrote about her in 1902, from an account that she wrote about Russell after his death and that was published in 1921 around the time of her own death and from a profile, and other references to her, in Katharine Tynan's *Memories* (1924).²

---

1. James H. Murphy, 'Rosa Mulholland,' *Cambridge Dictionary of Irish Biography*, dib-cambridge-org.
2. Matthew Russell, 'Poets I Have Known, VI, Rosa Mulholland,' *Donahoe's Magazine* 48:1 (1902), pp. 25–47; Rosa Mulholland, 'The Memoirs of Father Matthew Russell, SJ,' *Irish Monthly* (1921), 49:573, pp. 89–96; 49:574, pp. 133–40; 49:575, pp. 177–83; 49:576, pp. 221–7; 49:577, pp. 265–9; Katharine Tynan, 'Rosa Mulholland (Lady Gilbert), 1920,' in *Memories* (London: E. Nash and Grayson, 1924), pp. 305–22.

Rosa Mulholland had the oddest of nineteenth-century Irish backgrounds. She was a well-off Catholic from Ulster, a province with few centres of middle-class Catholic life. She was born in Belfast, where her father Joseph Stevenson Mulholland was a doctor. Her maternal grandparents were from Dublin and Connaught. She had a brother who became a judge, a sister, Clara, who became a children's author, and another sister, Ellen, who married Charles Russell (1832–1900), the legendary Irish barrister. He famously demolished the evidence of the man who had forged letters linking the Irish nationalist political leader, Charles Stewart Parnell (1846–91), with the revolutionary Fenians.[3] As Lord Russell of Killowen, he ended his career as Lord Chief Justice of England.

Killowen is an area in Co. Down on the northern shore of Carlingford Lough near Newry. The Russells lived between Killowen and Newry and the Russell and Mulholland families were friends. Rosa Mulholland often visited the Russells and grew close to Matthew Russell (1834–1912) whom she regarded as a big brother. Russell became a Jesuit priest and the founder, in 1873, and long-time editor (until his death in 1912), of the *Irish Monthly*, a magazine of literary and general interest for Catholics but also with a wider appeal.[4] Russell was one of the first to publish Oscar Wilde (1854–1900), for example.

When Mulholland was in her mid-teens her father died and her mother moved the family to Connemara in the west of Ireland. She had a desire to be an artist but had little opportunity while in the west to pursue painting and began instead to think about

---

3. Throughout the 1880s Parnell led the Irish Parliamentary Party in the Westminster parliament and pressed for Home Rule for Ireland. The conflict between landlords and tenants in Ireland took place at the same time and during it Parnell was accused of supporting the revolutionary Fenian organization, occasioning the investigation in which Russell represented Parnell.
4. Declan O'Keefe, 'A Man for Others and a Beacon in the Twilight: Matthew Russell, SJ, and the *Irish Monthly*,' *Studies*: 99:394 (2010), pp. 169–79.

writing. Later in her career her supporters credited her with having a special insight into the lives of the Irish peasantry and attributed this to her time living in Connemara.

For most of her adult life Mulholland was to live in Dublin, though with several lengthy stays in London. For the most part and until her marriage she lived with and was presumably supported by her relatives. In Dublin she lived with an aunt in Sherrard St, off Gardiner St. In London she stayed with her sister and the latter's husband in Harley St. One such stay, in the early 1860s, enabled her to study art for a while at the Kensington School of Art. Her first novel *Dunmara* was published in 1864 under the pseudonym Ruth Murray. One chapter and an extract from another chapter appear in this work. It is for the most part a standard romance but is remarkable for the description of its heroine's experience as an art student. This obviously draws on Mulholland's own experience. Equally remarkable is the heroine's debate with another student about feminism and on the degree to which women should be allowed to pursue careers, in this case in medicine, with the heroine's more cautious feminism pitted against that of her new friend's more radical stance. Though undoubtedly a cautious feminist herself Mulholland never shied away from giving voice to other views on the subject, enabling her work at times to be a locus for real dialogue.

The 1860s proved to be a remarkable decade for Mulholland as a young writer. In London she was befriended by perhaps the leading Victorian painter of the time, Sir John Millais (1829–96), who illustrated some of her published work, though her family induced her to turn down his offer to make her his pupil. Fiction was often published in magazines and throughout her career many of Mulholland's novels were published in magazines before they became books. Mulholland enjoyed a good deal of success in the London of the early 1860s, getting published in prestigious literary magazines. For example, the *Cornhill Magazine* published her poem, 'Irené', in 1862 and in the same year *London Society* published a short story based on her experience at art school.[5]

Mulholland's greatest success in the 1860s, however, came through her association with Charles Dickens (1812–70). He published short stories and poems by her and serialized her second and third novels, *Hester's History* (1869) and the *Wicked Woods of Tobereevil* (1872) in his own magazine, *All the Year Round*. When Tauchnitz, the German publisher of British writing, published *No Thoroughfare* (1867) by Dickens and Wilkie Collins (1824–89) in 1868, they included Mulholland's *The Late Miss Hollingford* (1886) with the volume, though her authorship was not credited and it was not published as a book under her name until 1886.

With Dickens's death in 1870 Mulholland began to shift away from London and moved towards Dublin where she was to live for the rest of her life. However, with no significant publishers of novels in Dublin she still published her books with London publishers and also continued to publish shorter pieces with London magazines. Four collections of Mulholland's short stories were published between the mid-1880s and mid-1890s, though often by Dublin publishers.[6]

Her short story, 'The Hungry Death', which is reproduced here, was published by *All the Year Round* in 1880 and was later

---

5. Rosa Mulholland, 'Irené,' *Cornhill Magazine* 5:28 (1862), 478–80; Rosa Mulholland, 'My First Picture,' *London Society* 1:4 (1862), 289–302. Mike Ashley, *The Age of the Storytellers: British popular fiction magazines, 1880–1950* (London: British Library and Oak Knoll Press, 2006). For more on women publishing in periodicals, on women writers and Irish women writers, see, for example, Kristine Moruzi, *Constructing Girlhood through the Periodical Press, 1850–1915* (Aldershot: Ashgate, 2012); Linda H. Peterson, *Becoming a Woman of Letters: Myths of Authorship and Facts of the Victorian Market* (Princeton, NJ: Princeton University Press, 2009); Whitney Standlee, *Power to Observe: Irish Women Novelists in Britain, 1890–1916* (Bern: Peter Lang, 2015).

6. Rosa Mulholland, *The Walking Trees, and Other Tales* (Dublin: Gill & Son, 1885); *The Haunted Organist of Hurly Burly, and Other Stories*. (London: Hutchinson [1891]). *Marigold and Other Stories* (Dublin, Eason & Son, 1894); *Our Own Story, and Other Tales* (London: Catholic Truth Society, [1896]).

chosen by W.B. Yeats for inclusion in his *Representative Irish Tales* (1891). It is of interest, not only as an example of Mulholland's extensive efforts in short fiction but because it deals with the famine. Scholarship on the famine in literature is a growing area and "The Hungry Death" is discussed by Marguérite Corporaal, for example, in *Relocated Memories: The Great Famine in Irish and Diaspora Fiction, 1846–1870*.[7]

However, it was in Dublin that Mulholland found a journal and an editor with whom she was to be associated for the rest of her career, the *Irish Monthly* and Matthew Russell. In looking back on the first twenty-five years of the magazine in 1897 Russell singled out Mulholland as a key figure without whom the magazine would not have survived and thrived.[8]

She published many short stories in the magazine and two of her most significant novels were serialized in it before they were published in book form, *The Wild Birds of Killeevy*, in the late 1870s, and *Marcella Grace* in 1885. The first was a very successful romance which was often praised for the positive view of Irish peasants it presented;[9] the second represented a major intervention in the genre of the land-war novel and three chapters from it are reproduced in this volume. The *Irish Monthly* published so much of Mulholland's work that someone once quipped that it ought to be renamed the *Irish Mulholland*. Matthew Russell was

---

7. Marguérite Corporaal, *Relocated Memories: The Great Famine in Irish and Diaspora Fiction, 1846–1870* (Syracuse, NY: Syracuse University Press, 2017), pp. 76, 79, 97. See also: C.T. Cusack, 'Sunk in the Mainstream. Irish Women Writers, Canonicity, and Famine Memory, 1892–1910,' in Kathryn Laing and Sinéad Mooney (eds.), *Irish Women's Writing at the Turn of the Twentieth Century. Alternative Histories, New Narratives* (Brighton: Edward Everett Root, 2020), pp. 37–48. 'The Hungry Death' is also reproduced in Marguérite Corporaal, C.T. Cusack and Lindsay Janssen (eds), *Recollecting Hunger: An Anthology. Cultural Memories of the Great Famine in Irish and British Fiction, 1847–1920* (Dublin: Irish Academic Press, 2012), pp. 234–42.
8. Matthew Russell, 'Silver Jubilee Retrospect,' *Irish Monthly* 25:283 (1897), pp. 1–6.
9. Murphy, *Catholic Fiction*, p. 33.

certainly very loyal to Mulholland. Shortly before his death he spoke of wanting to forgive an American Jesuit who had criticized Mulholland and her work.[10]

With an established presence in the British publishing market, a home base in Dublin and an outlet in the *Irish Monthly* Mulholland was able to create a balance that suited her as a writer, particularly of fiction. On the one hand, her work was acceptably Victorian and yet on occasion it promoted advanced views on the plight and role of women. On the other hand, it also presented a positive view of Catholics and occasionally a critique of Ireland's position in the British dispensation. Her audience was a general Victorian middle-class audience, though with a particular focus on Irish middle and upper-middle-class Irish Catholics such as herself. Her objectives when it came to both groups were largely similar. Upper-middle-class Irish Catholics wanted to be accepted as respectable Victorians. This involved modifying the British view of Ireland as lawless and its peasantry as violent.[11]

The 1880s saw often violent conflict between Irish landlords and tenants over rents and the ownership of land, with the government attempting to find solutions. Eventually, this resulted in small farmers becoming owners of their own farms. However, this solution was by no means clear when Mulholland wrote *Marcella Grace*, a novel that advocates the replacement of a Protestant landlord class with a class of Catholic landlords that might be more sympathetic to the tenantry, thus enabling the former to win the latter's support. The leading example of Catholic gentry fiction, it also raises the issue of a more active role for women in the public sphere of land ownership and politics. The novel provoked a riposte in the form of the anonymous *Priests and People: A No Rent Romance* (1891) which paints a less than

---

10. Katharine Tynan, 'Father Matthew Russell, SJ, a priest editor,' in *Memories*, pp. 145–60: pp. 150, 160.
11. James H. Murphy, *Catholic Fiction and Social Reality in Ireland, 1873–1922* (Westport CT: Greenwood, 1997), pp. 13–75.

positive view of the Irish tenantry. Both works were instances of land-war fiction, a polemical genre of the 1880s and 1890s in which contesting version of the land war and its possible solution were presented in fictional form by numerous authors, many of them women. They included Elizabeth Owens Blackburne, Wilkie Collins, M.E. Francis, Fannie Gallaher, Emily Lawless, Edna Lyall, Hannah Lynch, Letitia McClintock, George Moore, Edith Rochfort, Frances Mabel Robinson, W.P. Ryan, Somerville and Ross, Bram Stoker and Anthony Trollope.[12] *Marcella Grace* itself achieved such a stature that the leading Victorian novelist Mrs Humphrey (Mary Augusta) Ward (1851–1920) named one of her characters Marcella. *Marcella Grace* is perhaps Mulholland's most important book, combining her interests in Ireland, class, social respectability and women.

Mulholland wrote over thirty novels for adults and young readers over her career and four works specifically for children in the years around the late 1870s.[13] She was a popular writer though the absence of publishers' records make her sales hard to quantify. Her work was published in America as well as in Britain and Ireland. The land situation continued to be an issue in many of the works for adults. There was controversy in Sheffield, for example, when the school board there bought 200 copies of her 1889 novel, *Gianetta*, with its critical depiction of Irish landlords

---

12. Murphy, *Catholic Fiction*, pp. 20–1, 44–7; James H. Murphy, *Irish Novelists and the Victorian Age* (Oxford: Oxford University Press, 2011), pp. 167–92; Heidi Hansson and James H. Murphy (eds.), *Fictions of the Irish Land War* (Oxford: Peter Lang, 2014). For women and the land war see Heather Laird, 'Decentring the Irish land War: Women, Politics and the Private Sphere,' in Fergus Campbell and Tony Varley (eds), *Land Questions in Modern Ireland* (Manchester: Manchester University Press, 2013), pp. 175–93.

13. Rosa Mulholland, *The Little Flower Seekers, Being Adventures of Trot and Daisy in a Wonderful Garden by Moonlight* ([1873] London; Belfast: Marcus Ward & Co., 1880); *Five Little Farmers* (London: Belfast, Marcus Ward & Co., 1876); *Puck and Blossom, a Fairy Tale* (London; Belfast: Marcus Ward & Co., [1879]); *Four Little Mischiefs* (London: Blackie & Son, 1883).

and the cruelty of evictions of tenants.[14] As has been noted, her interest in the issue and in the life of the peasantry more generally was in part to do with a desire to make Ireland appear respectable in Victorian eyes. As a member of the upper-middle class Mulholland was aware that Victorian society perceived Ireland negatively in terms of the supposed behaviour of peasants. This related both to their engagement in political and agrarian agitation and also to their personal moral probity. Interestingly, many of the Catholic authors who formed part of the group clustered around the *Irish Monthly* tended to downplay specific Catholic issues in order to appear more acceptably Victorian, as the latter's norms derived from a more Protestant worldview. Mulholland was not one of them and in this respect, as with her writing on the land situation, she took the risk of alienating parts of her audience.

In one novel, *Nanno, a Daughter of the State* (1899), three of whose chapters are reproduced here, Muholland tackles head on the difference between the Victorian Protestant world-view in which respectability, once lost, can never be recovered and the Catholic worldview in which forgiveness and a new start are possible. Her novel tries to solve the tension by allowing that a woman who has a child out of wedlock might be forgiven but that she still must face the certainty that, were she to be honest about it, no respectable man would marry her. That this was a controversial area is attested to by the fact that Ellen O'Leary (1831–89), poet and sister of the Fenian leader John O'Leary (1830–1907), had objected to an earlier story by Mulholland in which a girl from a workhouse, a state institution in which poor people might reside, marries a farmer. "'An Irish farmer would not marry a girl like that; an English farmer might.'"[15] By the early twentieth century the drive for British approval was in general decline. The Mulholland novel that perhaps comes closest to an assertion of the positive role of the Catholic faith is *Father Tim* (1910). Here the emphasis

---

14. Murphy, *Catholic Fiction*, p. 41.
15. Katharine Tynan, 'John and Ellen O'Leary,' in *Memories*, pp. 91–109: p. 97.

is on the positive role of the Church in the area of temperance, with Tim stressing that the moral character of Irish people derives from their religious faith in a novel that spans both the rural and the urban.

Over time Mulholland's interest in gender shifted from a concern with women in professional roles or as landlords (as in *Dunmara* and *Marcella Grace*) to a concern with women towards the bottom of the socio-economic scale, as with *Nanno*. Among her final novels were works such as *The Return of Mary O'Murrough* (1908), three of whose chapters are reproduced here, that deal with the position of women in the economic reality of the Ireland of small farmers that had emerged in the wake of the land war.[16] In this world women had to be both attractive in a traditional way and yet also economically generative, with the latter often being at the cost of the former. At the very least, this novel shows that Mulholland was capable of adapting to changed times. And, as ever, she notes the interconnectedness of economics and gender. This was of course also a theme pursued by other novels, such as Emily Lawless in *Grania* (1892), the story of a young island woman struggling towards self-definition as she negotiates her need to make a living with the unsatisfactory marriage choice available to her.

In addition to her fiction Mulholland published short, occasional pieces in the *Irish Monthly* on a variety of themes that included religious topics, biography and travel, as well as several short plays. In the latter part of her career she also wrote improving pamphlets for young people for the London-based Catholic Truth Society and for the Catholic Truth Society of Ireland. The *Irish Monthly* generated a literary circle and culture whose achievements and possibilities have been overlooked in the attention given to the Anglo-Irish Literary Revival that developed

---

16. "'She's nothin' but a shadda": The Politics of Marriage in Late Mulholland,' in Anna Pilz and Whitney Standlee (eds.), *Advancing the Cause of Liberty: Irish Women's Writing, 1878–1922* (Manchester: Manchester University Press, 2016), pp. 33–48.

a short time after it, hence their subsequent neglect. Mulholland was certainly a prominent member of the group, though she is believed to have had a serious falling out at one stage with another leading member, Katharine Tynan (1859–1931).

The row seems to have been about a piece that Tynan wrote about Sir Charles Russell in which she said, based on something Matthew Russell had said to her, that his family, with its middle-class Ulster, Catholic origins, was related to the Russells who were Dukes of Bedford. The Russells apparently thought this made them seem like snobs and they cold-shouldered Tynan and Rosa Mulholland wrote her a letter which she said 'made me very unhappy.'[17]

In 1891 a piece by Mulholland, entitled, 'Wanted an Irish Novelist' and reproduced here, was published in the magazine. She called on Irish writers to write about Ireland rather than for the English market. Though she had herself made a choice about living in and writing about Ireland she was also financially in a much more favourable position than many of her contemporaries, who were forced to meet market demand in order to survive. She had lived in family homes all her life and that year was to marry a rather well-off scholar.[18]

Finally, it is important also to note that Mulholland was an impressive poet, collecting her verse in three volumes over a seventeen-year period towards the end of her career.[19] Selections from these books are reproduced here. Hitherto, there has been

17. Tynan, Katharine. 'Lord Russell of Killowen, Lord Chief Justice of England,' in *Memories*, pp. 47–58: p. 53.
18. For the difficult circumstances of other novelists see Murphy, *Irish Novelists*, pp. 245–60.
19. Rosa Mulholland, *Vagrant Verses* (London: Elkin Mathews, [1899]); *Spirit and Dust. Poems* (London: Elkin Mathews, 1908); *Dreams and Realities* (London; Edinburgh, Sands & Co., 1916). George O'Neill, 'The Poetry of Rosa Mulholland, Lady Gilbert,' *Irish Monthly* 49:580 (1921), pp. 397–405. For a recent general study of the area, though it does not include Mulholland, see: Lucy Collins (ed.), *Poetry by Women in Ireland: A Critical Anthology 1870–1970* (Liverpool: Liverpool University Press, 2012).

no real attention to this aspect of her work, though it ranges from the devotional to the anguished and even to the political, with Mulholland moving at one point beyond the rural to consider the challenges facing women in an industrial setting.

In 1891, aged fifty, Rosa Mulholland married the Dublin historian John T. Gilbert (1829–98). They lived at Villa Nova in Blackrock, Co. Dublin. She became Lady Gilbert when he was knighted and wrote a biography of him, as well as editing some of his unfinished work when he died.[20] She also helped publish the work of her late friend Sarah Atkinson (1823–93), a writer and biographer and member of the *Irish Monthly* circle who had worked to alleviate the plight of poor women in Dublin.

Tynan's profile, published after Mulholland's death, reflects the complex relationship between her and Mulholland, one in which early admiration on Tynan's part had given way to something like antagonism, as, in Tynan's view, she had grown in distinction as a writer and even eclipsed her mentor without receiving proper recognition from Mulholland. Tynan sees all Mulholland's relationships in terms of dominance and submission. Mulholland had a 'dominant character' but was, nonetheless, submissive to her family and to older friends such as Sarah Atkinson. Her dominant relatives, whom Tynan does not specifically name, had prevented her from marrying when she was young: 'She was really a dark Rose who had been surrounded by briars against her lovers.' When she did eventually marry, it was a love match but she was already middle-aged and never became a mother: 'If she had had both in youth she might not have lacked suavity: she might not have been rigid as she came to be in her enclosed convent garden of life with the high walls built round it.' In Tynan's view, she was emotionally repressed: 'No nun could have been half so much afraid of passion as she was.'

---

20. Rosa Mulholland, *Life of Sir John T. Gilbert, LL.D., F.S.A., Irish Historian and Archivist, Vice-President of the Royal Irish Academy, Secretary of the Public Records Office of Ireland* (London: Longmans and Co., 1905).

For Tynan, Mulholland's religiosity was compensatory and excessive. On one occasion the two of them travelled to see New Tipperary, a settlement for evicted tenants, with a view to writing about it for the newspapers. Tynan recalled that Mulholland brought out holy pictures and a votive lamp in their hotel room. 'I can remember a time when it was my dream to be her handmaiden,' was Tynan's sardonic comment. Tynan resented still being treated as a child by Mulholland at social occasions in London. She believed that Mulholland disapproved of her support for the fallen Irish political leader Parnell, on account of his involvement in a divorce case. Tynan further believed that John T. Gilbert did not like her and that 'perhaps it was a vicarious literary jealousy on Rosa's behalf.' In the end Tynan returned to her theme: 'I remember her saying once that the strength of my will terrified her, but it was only that my will had resisted hers.' Their relationship was an odd one of affection and wariness. Tynan said that she never revealed her full self to Mulholland, but that when Mulholland was angry with her it was anger with someone she loved. As Mulholland wrote no memoir of her own, we are left to sift the truth in Tynan's bruised reminiscences. Certainly, though, Mulholland's early promise in London gave way to a more conventional later life in Dublin.[21] But, on the other hand, Mulholland's writing at times evidences a far from timid and repressed approach. The women who populate her novels are not at all compliant. They are often clear sighted and determined in the face of considerable difficulties and obstacles. Perhaps the inner Mulholland was not entirely the person whom Tynan observed. Perhaps, too, Mulholland had not entirely revealed herself to Tynan.

Mulholland's death coincided with Irish independence, and her work largely ceased to be read and was mostly forgotten. She returned to critical attention from the 1990s, thanks to the work of the editor of the current volume, both in particular studies and

---

21. Tynan, 'Rosa Mulholland,' pp. 306, 312, 317, 321.

in his two general assessments of Irish fiction, *Catholic Fiction and Social Reality in Ireland, 1873–1922* (1997) and *Irish Novelists and the Victorian Age* (2011).[22] My approach was initially one of class, seeing Mulholland as one of the principal authors from an upper-middle-class Catholic background who were keen to present a version of Ireland consonant with their own class perspective during the era of the land war, and who were the predominant voices in Irish fiction from the founding of the *Irish Monthly* until the 1890s, when they were overtaken by Catholic intelligentsia writers, who were critical of society in a new way. From the beginning, however, I recognized that gender was a central issue for Mulholland. Indeed, her interest in class was related to her interest in gender. In *Marcella Grace*, for example, the heroine's more assertive posture is seen as determined by the destabilized economic situation. In my later work, I went on to focus more specifically on gender in Mulholland's work, both in her earliest novel, *Dunmara*, and in her late work in which poorer women and peasant women face issues of gender, economics and social and religious expectations. Other scholars, such as Heidi Hansson, have also explored Mulholland's depictions of lone, struggling women.[23]

As well as gender, class, religion, economics and, indeed as has been noted above, famine, Mulholland's fiction has also been referenced in terms of the New Girl and New Woman.[24] Equally,

---

22. For details of these studies see the Select Bibliography.
23. Heidi Hansson, 'From Reformer to Sufferer: The Returning Exile in Rosa Mulholland's Fiction,' in Michael Böss, Irene Gilsenan Nordin and Britta Oinder (eds.), *Re-Mapping Exile: Realities and Metaphors in Irish Literature and History* (Aarhus: Aarhus University Press, 2006), pp 89–106.
24. Susan Cahill. 'Making Spaces for the Irish Girl: Rosa Mulholland and Irish Girls in Fiction at the turn of the Century,' in Kristine Moruzi and Michelle J. Smith (eds.) *Colonial Girlhood in Literature, Culture and History, 1840–1950* (London: Palgrave Macmillan, 2014), pp. 167–79; Tina O'Toole, *The Irish New Woman* (Basingstoke: Palgrave Macmillan, 2013); Faith Binckes and Kathryn Laing, *Hannah Lynch (1859–1904): Irish writer, Cosmopolitan, New Woman* (Cork: Cork University Press, 2019).

her work in horror fiction has both been studied and recently anthologized.[25] Undoubtedly, much remains to be explored in the writing of Rosa Mulholland not only in terms of her fiction but also in relation to her poetry and non-fiction.

---

25. Richard Dalby, 'Rosa Mulholland, Mistress of the Macabre,' *The Green Book: Writings on Irish Gothic, Supernatural and Fantastic Literature*, 9 (2017), pp. 19–23; Richard Dalby (ed.), *Not to Be Taken at Bed-Time and Other Strange Stories by Rosa Mulholland* (Dublin: Swan River Press, 2019).

1

From *Dunmara*.
3 vols. London, Smith Elder, 1864.

(under the pseudonym Ruth Murray)

Volume Three: Chapters Three and Eleven [extract].

Introduction

The first two volumes of the novel offer a conventional story of the adventures of a young woman making her way in the world, who is the object of an improbable coincidence that links her with her previously unknown early life and background. Ellen Wilde is washed ashore in Ireland after a shipwreck and is taken in by the Aungiers of Dunmara House where her late mother had once been a ward of old Mr Aungier. She ends the novel by marrying a member of the family. However, in the interim she lives in London, studies art and discovers that her father, known as Mr. Waldron, is in fact alive. He helps her financially.

In Volume Three, Chapter Three, Ellen Wilde arrives in London and becomes a student at the West End Academy, near the Kensington attic where she lives. Mulholland's account undoubtedly relies on her own time as a student at the art school in South Kensington that would later become the Royal College of Art and which was located close to the South Kensington Museum (now the Victoria and Albert Museum). Ellen Wilde is initially put in a room to sketch plaster casts of gods from the Greco-Roman world. She later moves to another room where she has a conversation with wealthy Felicia Rothwell. She has more pronouncedly feminist views than Ellen, who wishes to blend women's professional advancement (in a career as an artist, for example) with the retention of traditional feminine attributes. One of Rothwell's ambitions was to become a doctor and she had considered going to Philadelphia, USA, where there was a women's medical college. This is a notion that Ellen Wilde finds strange. In fact, the year after the publication of *Dunmara*, Elizabeth Garrett Anderson (1836–1917) became the first qualified, openly-female doctor in Britain, though regulations were tightened and no further women doctors were recognized until 1876.

Volume Three, Chapter Eleven, sees Ellen Waldron, as she is now known, living comfortably in London with her ailing father, who dies at the end of the chapter. In the extract from the chapter included here Ellen once more discusses art with Felicia. Whereas Felicia's goal is women's independence, Ellen's valuing of art comes second to her commitment to family and, indeed, becomes a way of recovering family.

In spite, or perhaps even because of, its intriguing content, *Dunmara* did not make much of an impact and was never listed among the novels for which Mulholland was best known. Indeed, in 1905 the *Irish Monthly* actually republished it in serial form in a unique reversal of the accustomed publication process. When this editor initially located a copy of the original edition in the British Library he found that the pages were uncut.

CHAPTER THREE
STUDIES IN THE ACADEMY

The West End Academy was not far distant from the Kensington attic, and Ellen had no great difficulty in obtaining admission as a student of the female school. For the first week she went and came, speaking to no one and bending over her drawing-board, intent upon her work. A place had been assigned her in the most remote of several small rooms opening from a long, large hall. Here she made outlines of the casts that hung about. Now it was a brawny foot, and now my lady's dimpled arm, clasped with a dainty bracelet. Now it was two trusting hands clasped with a truthful energy that creased the snowy plaster like flesh. Or it was a little baby's sleeping face reposting on the wrinkles of its chubby neck; or the pure drooping profile of a Psyche, or an agonized mask of the Laocoön.[1] At the end of the first week the world of new bustling life which had been surging around her for six days was still strange, while the white world of the statuesque had grown oppressively familiar.

It forced upon the silent student a wearing self-consciousness. Each stony face had its suggestion to make, its sermon to preach, its question to ask, but not one would accept of a response. The agony in yonder tortured plaster mocked eternally mere human troubles that passed away. And that noble Apollo, gazing sunward with his splendid smile, magnificent in his haughty perfection, with what radiant contempt he turned his stately head from the anxious eyes that drooped all day before his accomplished majesty, and mused upon his own glory as the underlying creation of immortal genius.[2] Serenely conscious of the busy thoughts that clustered around their white intelligence, not a lip nor an eyelid would wake from its grand dream of concentration. "Persist!" said their silence. "Each of us in the petrification of one idea, and in the gilding of its own completeness is therefore stamped 'perfect for all ages'."

"Hands of stone," ran Ellen's thought, "what do you mean by your vehement clasp? What passion wrought in the soul whose power of will constrained you? Are you praying for life, or are you imploring death? Are you giving rapturous thanks, or is it despair that starts the full veins so, and imbeds the little fingers in the white flesh?" They will not answer, and Ellen, blindly feeling

---

1. Psyche was the Greek goddess of the soul. Laocoön was a Trojan priest and the subject of a famous classical sculpture in the Vatican Museum.
2. Apollo was the Greek god of the sun.

her way to the pulse that stains palm to palm, curves here, and straightens there, and strives to render their true meaning, while the sun comes and spreads a pool of shadow beneath them, and sets fingers with rings of gold.

"Pretty Psyche," she muses on, "will you stand there for ever on your bracket with your childish beauty and your innocent smile? Will you never weep? What right do you have to keep your youth and your sweet gladness undimmed as a crystal through all the destroying years of a world for sunshine only ripens to furnish decay with a harvest. Happy Psyche, no summer can mature you! Provoking Psyche, no blast can play you! But then you are only the petrification of an idea, a beautiful piece of frost. You serve no purpose but to make people glad when they are already happy, and to tease them when they are not. I wish I could turn my back upon your prettiness, but then I should have to sacrifice this excellent light, and that would be inconvenient."

"When I must look up again I will glance to the noble Dian who is robing for the chase yonder on her pedestal.[3] There is no purpose, there is action. No sadly drooping hair fans her slim cheek with suggestions of drowsiness; it is gathered from brow and ear, lest mischievous winds, in some breathless moment, laughingly blind her with a tress. Her ankles are sandalled as with strength and fleetness, her arm is curved in the unconscious pride of grace; a look of simple dignity crowns the queenly beauty of her countenance. By her is her quiver of goodly arrows. They will presently bring down from on high that at which the huntress wills to aim. Some of these shafts will miss, and fall to the ground. The archeress knows it. Will she then lay down her bow and languish with disappointment while the stag rushes on hand through the forest? No; there are no arrows yet, staunch and swift, to fly and pierce. Clasp your mantle and speed, brave Dian! There is no haze upon that fearless eye. You should laugh and count

---

3. Diana was the Greek goddess of hunting.

your spoils heaped about your knees. When I have to look up I will study your grand simplicity, and the study will be profitable as a sermon."

"I wish someone would take that mask of Bacchus and hang its ugliness at the other side of the pillar.[4] Poor disfigured face! can you not find some friendly god to loosen that bandage of serrated leaves, and fling back the colossal curls from your brows? It were better, if you must have a crown, that you had bound your manly locks with the water-lily, I think. I hate the sight of your stolid eyes and thick lips."

"Wise Minerva, what a reproach to foolish folk like me gleams in the sovereign gravity of your fair face![5] Are you very much satisfied either with the young lady of the hard black eyes and mechanical wit, whose conversation has been rattling on my ear, like hailstones on the roof, ever since early morning? She is taking great pains to round your face nicely with shadows in sepia, and meanwhile she is talking to that other young lady who is giving to the world a representation of some very purple raisins reposing upon a very green table-cover beside an exceedingly rosy-cheeked apple. She talks with the air of one who has sifted the world to the bottom, and knows to a grain of sand all it contains. She dashes at her opinions and flings them from her as if she had spent all her life in learning them off by heart in paragraphs. She winds up her sentences with a flourish, as if one took a long breathless race, and whirling around at the end made an abrupt "cheese" with one's skirts, just to show how little the exertion had disturbed one. What is she talking about? I can still hear with one ear, but I require two to understand with. Do you think she's really studying to learn the tricks of your sober mouth and far-seeing eye, Minerva? Heigho! You begin to oppress me, you queer white people who know all my secrets. I cannot have you playing ghost at me forever, I think that next week I will either place some flesh

---

4. Bacchus was the Roman god of wine.
5. Minerva was the Roman goddess of wisdom.

and blood barriers between you and me, or else I will escape to another room altogether. There goes the bell! Adieu till Monday."

In the new room to which Ellen was speedily transferred, there was less of plaster and more of flesh and blood. The eternal flow of the "strong"-minded young lady's eloquence was heard no more, but a low hum of several voices speaking in a subdued key filled, without annoying her ears. At times even this hum ceased and the room was very quiet. Ellen was pleased with the new atmosphere.

There were many students. There was a brisk little elderly lady in grey curls and a bonnet, who was working studiously at a board much higher than herself. There was a pleasant-looking young lady in a black silk and holland apron, who was painting geraniums from nature. There were tall girls in short socks and broad girls in tight frocks. There were stupid faces and intelligent faces, there were hard workers and idlers. There were plain dresses, and there were gay and rich ones, which looked out of place in a room with chalk and paint. The lady mistress, a gentle creature with shining brown hair and a soft step and voice, is at present flitting from one student to another, giving words of encouragement or advice. Now she has finished with this room and vanishes elsewhere.

Many eyes are on Ellen as she enters, with the soft somber folds of her black cashmere dress falling long and graceful to the matting, a scrap of blue ribbon tied under her tiny white collar, her gold brown hair brushed back from her clear face and knotted in a mass of braids behind. She is observed, and commented on in whispers (not rudely), and then the "new student" is for the time forgotten.

When her cheek has cooled from the first flush of shyness, she glances around and makes the observations which we have already made. Her nearest neighbour is perched up on a tall seat, with the pins of her easel placed in the highest holes. She is shading in chalk the bust of the massive Venus, and is looking at it across the top of Ellen's easel.[6]

---

6. Venus was the Roman goddess of beauty.

Ellen looks up to her once or twice and is attracted. She is a pale, fair, thoroughly English-looking girl, with faint gold hair, parted evenly over her smooth full forehead, and coming in tiny rings of curls to the edge of a collar behind. This style of hair-dressing exposes the outline of her well-shaped head, and a coronet of black velvet gives a sort of classic Minerva-like expression to the profile turned towards Ellen. There is a slight air of haughtiness in the intent preoccupation of her brows, and a large degree of resolution about her somewhat pale mouth. Her dress of soft dark green contrasts brilliantly with her complexion, Ellen thinks it a remarkable figure, statuesque from the artistic, patrician from the everyday point of view. She would do for the heroine of a Norse legend —[7]

> When of old Hilderbrand
> I asked his daughter's hand.[8]

Fancy rang out the chimes in Ellen's ears, but common sense stayed her presently with, "Nonsense, all this is not improving the nose of your Bacchante!"[9]

Presently a shower of bread-crumb comes raining down from the skirts of the Norse heroine into Ellen's lap. Involuntarily Ellen looks up, and the Norse young lady looks down.

"I beg your pardon!" The blonde face is smiling down from out of its pale gold framework. I hope it did not fall in your eyes."

"No!" Ellen smiles responsive, and that is all the prices between them for the present.

When the bell rings the students troop off as usual to the luncheon-room. Ellen and her neighbour remain alone among the deserted easels. The blonde young lady, without dismounting

---

7. Referring to the Norsemen or Vikings, warrior peoples from Scandinavia during the European dark ages. They were supposedly tall and blond haired.
8. From 'The Skeleton in Armour' by Henry Wadsworth Longfellow (1807–82).
9. A follower of Bacchus.

from her perch, unties a little paper parcel, takes the scarlet book from the shelf beside her, and spreading it upon her knees begins to read, while she eats some slices of brown bread and butter, Ellen meanwhile, too anxious to think of pausing, works on with her chalk, conscious of nothing but the tedious process of rounding a plaster cheek in strong shadow.

At last she desists a moment, looks around the empty room, and finally glances up at her solitary neighbour; thereupon she meets the gaze of two observant pale blue eyes. The Norse heroine is looking down from a high place, and she says,

"Do you mean to keep up that rate of working? Will you never draw breath?"

Ellen tries to smile but she is very tired and leans back wearily.

"Oh! I don't know. I have not any time to lose."

"I see; but you will defeat your purpose. Why do you study? Do you mean to be an artist?"

Ellen widens her eyes slightly. "Of course I do."

"Ah! We all say that, but we mean so many different things. Have you any ideas of your own?"

"I should hope so." (Laughing).

"Don't laugh at me, please; I am in earnest; you cannot think how scarce those articles are here. Do you ever put yours up on paper?"

"Yes, and upon canvas; too often, I fear, for my own good. The stern white task-work comes dry after a long enjoyment of a free pencil in Fancyland."

"Ah, I see you understand me; not half a dozen in this place would speak in that strain. I observed a little sleepy-looking girl, the other day, who had just entered the school. Miss Lowndes asked her what her purpose was in coming here to study. She hung her head aside with a little simper, and said, 'I want to be an artist.' She ought to have added, 'I place myself in your hands and expect to be put through the process somehow.' I have watched the girl since, she has as much imagination as a buttercup."

"Well," Ellen said, "I have been struck by the spirit of industry prevalent here. Everyone seems so earnest over her work."

"Earnest over her work so far as it goes; but her idea of her own is low. The stone is a stone; and a statue is only a stone cold and polished to a pretty shape. The Dian is nothing more but a graceful isolated form. They painted her no background of skies at dawn. They clear her no paths in the forest tickets. The standard of art is made light and set low, that the weakest or most audacious may lift and plant it where they please. It is desecration."

"I think you are hardly fair. Enthusiasm blinds you a little. Art is a beautiful tree with low branches that trail to the earth and look graceful, making pleasant shade on hot roads, as well as with the high plumes that swing against the blue and toss the golden apples in the sun. Those who cannot touch the fruit, or even smell the blossoms, why may they not pick the green leaves below to garnish their homes; or even to flavour insipid food? Because you are a good climber yourself, you should not grudge their humbler portion to the less fortunate."

"You have made a mistake there. I am not a good climber. I do see those golden apples of yours between the bows, just when wayward breezes choose to show them to me. I have glimpses of ideas, but the climbing difficulty is precisely mine at present."

"Look here!" said of the Norse young lady, abruptly producing a piece of drawing paper. "Here is almost the first original sketch I have ever attempted. You perceive how crude it is. Observe how awkwardly that old man sits in his chair. And the girl will persist in wearing a mask in spite of all my efforts to coax her to show me her true face. Yet I see it all here," she said, tapping her fair full brow. "I have got a bit of ore, but it is so clogged with rubbish, that it is at present more a burden to me than a prize."

"How long have you studied to be an artist?" asked Ellen, examining the sketch.

"Not long. It is a little more than a year since I first thought of it. That surprises you?"

"Yes. I thought that your kind of feeling was always born with one."

The pale-gold head was shaking slowly, that pale-blue eyes were fixed abstractly upon the matting.

"No," she said. "Something was born with me. I had got a thing to do and power to do it. I could not find it out at first. I tried several things. I wanted to be a doctor at one time. I had made up my mind. Some friends would have taken me with them to Philadelphia, but my mother implored me to give it up, I am her only daughter, and I did so."

"I think she was right. What an independent person you are. A female doctor! – What a strange idea!"

"Why so strange? I had got hands, and a brain, and because I happened to have been cast in a feminine mould, those hands and that brain were considered to have full, satisfactory, and most honourable occupation, whilst their owner whirled night after night round the floor of a ball-room at the pleasure of any coxcomb who chose to make her his bow. I was perfectly sick of the life we girls had to lead. It is nothing at the best but dressing, and dancing, and flirting; and flirting, and dancing, and dressing. I said I would not submit to it."

"When I gave up the Philadelphia idea, I thought all at once that, perhaps, I should find my work waiting me upon an easel, and so I coaxed mama to come to London for a few years. She hardly approved of my notions. She thinks a woman never should come forward in any way. I think the reverse. Why should not woman give herself to a high calling, as well as man? Why should she not work the powers she has got? I think the greater numbers of idle creatures who find work, the better for the world."

"I think so. But could you find no work at home?"

"No: there was nothing particular to be done, and if there had been, I could not have done it."

"I am not like you there. I love all kinds of home duties. I like charming a room into order and harmony. I like making a brilliant hearth, I like playing housewife and getting tea ready. I believe that rather than be an iceberg of a woman, I'd spend my life in washing children's faces!"

"Why, who is enthusiastic now? You quite blaze out. You are much cooler about your golden apples."

"Does that seem unnatural? The difference between art and a tea cup is the difference between the intellect and the domestic instincts. They may keep quite near, and one may help the other. If I were living in a palace of high art with nothing to do but to soar to the seventh heaven of fancy, from morning till night, I should find myself lonely in the midst of it all, for a little bit of sewing to do, or a child on my knees to talk nonsense."

"Queer! You seem to have got two distinct natures in you. That is not common. I cannot understand it. I cannot conceive one with your tastes and aspirations stooping to such common-place trifles which you share with the silliest of womankind."

Said Ellen, "I know how you feel. I can see with your eyes, but I believe you too have a defect of vision of which you will one day be conscious. I don't think any woman is justified, or that she is studying her own interests, when she ignores the small humble charities and duties of life. In the comparison with men, she puts herself at a disadvantage, for strive as she will, she can never arrive at the masculine summit of intellectual power. The finest degree of the one kind will always overtop the finest degree of the other kind. Why then, if she must accept her inferiority with one hand, will she not hold forth her other hand filled to overflowing with that superiority which is her own? Why will she contemptuously put out that rare soft lamp, which shines brightest in her show of lights, and to which men's coarse glare gives out no corresponding ray? I think it is well with the woman who has no existence out of the world of love and charity. And next to her, I think it is well with the woman who, having sterner inspirations given by Providence for a purpose, can turn on the instant from easel, chisel, or pen, not disgusted and reluctant, but gladly, cheerfully, to do even such common place things as tending a sick bed, or darning a child's stocking. Even the most isolated life has need of such calls. Obedience to them entails increase of liberty, and for those who live among their kind they are never ceasing. What would you do?" Ellen says, finishing off her long speech with an arched glance — "what would become of you if the fates appointed marriage to be your portion in life? What a thrifty wife you would be, sitting up in your high tower holding converse with the muses and disdaining to think of what was going to be for dinner!"

"The fates shall never play me such a trick as that," said the Norse young lady, with a grave emphasis, "I will never marry. There is not a man in existence who is worth the sacrifice of a woman's life. A wife is only a slave. When a man has got his dinner, he wants nothing more of you. You may go and wash the dishes, if you please; only give him his cigar and newspaper, and don't disturb him till it is time to go to the club or play. No, I shall never marry, certainly no one who could not indulge all my tastes and allow me to enjoy the life I covet."

Ellen's head stirs disapprovingly as she thoughtfully carves at her piece of chalk.

"You don't agree with me. I suppose not. I read 'dreamer' in your eyes. I dare say you could sketch me in some pretty pictures of 'love in a cottage' with a maid-of-all-work in the background spilling your 'medium' over the carpet."

"If you want such an entertainment you must seek it elsewhere!" Ellen retorted with a girlish pique. "I am no more given to silly sentimentalism than you are. Nevertheless," she added, "I will say so much as this. The question, as I should view it, would be, 'Did I like the man well enough to spend my life with him anywhere?' That well answered, the 'where' would be a small consequence. A cottage would do quite as well as any place else. I say this, because I think it is the right view to take of things, though I am as little likely to marry, perhaps less so, than you are."

Ellen's cheeks are hot, and she begins fanning herself vigorously, though somewhat ineffectually, with a large end of a T square. The Norse young lady sits quietly looking at her, till the reluctant eyes are forced to raise themselves a little haughtily to those other ones of pale blue above. Then the blonde face breaks out into another of it smiles, smiles remarkable for exceeding sweetness and womanliness, which comes forth shyly, as if they had escaped from control, and were doubtful about the consequences; smiles which are invariably kept in check by a certain shadow of reservation in the eyes, a cool preoccupation which never gives way, even when mirth curves the calm lips, and dimples the fair cheeks with a temporary pinkness.

"You and I are not like young ladies apt to make confidences, are we?" she says with her smile. "By the way," she adds, abruptly, "if we sit here together, we still have to speak sometimes. What shall I call you?"

Ellen silently pointed to her name in the corner of her drawing board.

"And here is my name," says the Norselander, lifting the corner of her scarlet book. Ellen reads "Felicia Rothwell."

"Now we know one another," says Felicia.

"A little," (with a doubtful look).

"Lo! here are the troops returning with forces replenished to make a fresh attack upon the citadel of art. There is private Mary Blank, who 'wants to be' a general. Oh! you sleepy girl, go home!"

CHAPTER ELEVEN [EXTRACT]
FELICIA'S BALL

Returned to London, Ellen's life entered a new phase. She dusted up the old studio, and arranged it after her own fancy. Here, pencil in hand, she spent long hours, scribbling on a block with the yellow book open at some favourite scene before her. The difficulties which she had to deal with in making her illustrations, kept her blood flowing, and carried her busily on from day to day. She entered into it. Sometimes it was sweet and quick, her pencil flowed with a facile power, and she went about the house with a serene brow and eyes full of a glorious spiritual joy. Her feet on those days seemed to tread on air. Spells of distrust in herself would come when all her conceptions seemed commonplace and conventional, and when her execution seemed full of feminine feebleness. And obstacles would arise in scenes hard to translate into picture, when, soaring with the author, seeing with his vision, and growing strong with his power, she yet seemed to feel blindly for forms grand enough, and subtleties of aspect fresh enough, in which to give to his words a visible shape. At these times she would leave a pencil and book, and pace up and down the gallery; and, rallying every power within her, she would meet and wrestle with her difficulties, till by dint of concentration she compelled them to give way, sometimes by slow degrees, sometimes at the bursting forth of a sudden light. "I have got it at last," she would say, and hasten down to the studio, and dash off her sketch. "My pencil is free again. Ah, here is a sweet face. How is it that I have drawn anything so lovely? I shall love that little countenance always. I hope the engraver will not alter a single stroke or curve."

"I think my hero's attitude will do now. The turn of his head satisfies me. It is manly. How I did worry over that yesterday, and now it comes right enough. Where have I got this bit of landscape? Where was I standing by those old trees, and one ray of light coming through them and eddying down, down amongst the sagons, crowding together in that still pool, and down, down into its black water? I have been there, but whether in the flesh or in a dream, one of my old real-like dreams, I cannot remember. I like this drawing. I do like it. Come, bundle up, and get burnt, all the rest of you wretched scrawled candidates for this important office, the office of visual interpreter to a majestic being called Eloquence, of a race rarer than kings."

"There, Ellen Waldron, you would remain for hours gloating over your two or three paltry (mock?) jewels that you have grubbed out of the rubbishing soil of your own brain, and you would sit fretting and altering at their settings, as if you, conceited thing, expected ever to achieve a perfect necklace of perfect gems! There, hurry them all past and make off. Your father will need you by the time you have assumed your nice silk dress, in which you enjoy to feel yourself so much the lady, and have fetched your work-basket, and set the first stitch in your embroidery."

The blocks were all ready at last. The engraver was satisfied, and in due course of time the illustrated edition of the book called *Sunward* was published.[10]

Summer had worn away by that time, and it was the autumn. The time of Ellen's departure with her father and Maud was coming near. The Drummond boys had left the Largie for school. Maud would be in London before a great many weeks. Meanwhile a startling event suspended all the arrangements. Mr. Waldron got a stroke of paralysis, and lay for weeks hovering between life and death. Even after the immediate danger passed away, he continued in so helpless a state that it seemed very doubtful whether he would be able to move abroad during the coming winter.

Ellen was unfailing in her attendance on him. Pencils were forgotten as though such things had never been. The studio was again without a tenant. Sitting by her father's bedside, reading to him, writing for him, or doing a little sewing; so her time passed. The evenings were getting very short now, and the dusk came quickly into the large old front bedroom where Mr. Waldron lay. There, when the firelight began to leap over the old green velvet arm-chair by the hearth, and to flit into the corners of the room, flinging strange grotesque shadows from the heavy, pillared bed, Ellen would vividly recall the evenings so long ago, when at such

---

10. Ellen Waldron has been illustrating a book whose author turns out to be the member of the Aungier family she eventually marries.

an hour, and in such a red glimmer as this, she had reaped her harvest of still warm delight in the west room at Dunmara.

She would sit down on the hearthrug with her hands in her lap, and think, "Dunmara, old house, how do you look, within and without? I can see the grey serried hills beyond your chimneys. I see the rain-clouds mustering above their peaks. I hear the seething of the tide; it will have wrought itself into fury by twelve o'clock to-night. I see within the dim hall; dining-room and drawing-room are dim also; the library door is shut, and a streak of light is lying beneath it. I see the wide stairs, with the pale moon splotching the queer old carved balustrades with white. She will not live long, that moon; a rushing torrent of clouds will presently drown her."

"Mrs. Kirker's lamp burns on her table. She has begun by now to close the painted shutters over her latticed window of nights. There are no blossoms on the geraniums. Blank west room, there is no dreamer nestling on your hearth. There is a new coffin in the vault at the ruin. Hark, the wind! If I do not rouse up, I shall fancy that I hear the great beech-tree striking the window. I shall forget that there is a street outside. Ah, there is an organ to break the spell. Why do these organs make me cry? I don't know. It is jingling a merry air. Never was anything so melancholy."

The organ goes, and the abstraction comes back. To drive it away, Ellen glides to the window, and sits down amongst the curtains. She watches the opposite house, seeing the servant come in, to light the chandeliers in the drawing-room. She gets a peep into a bright scene as the light springs up suddenly, and the figures in the room rise and move about. There are young ladies in their floating evening dresses, there is a nice elderly mamma in her elegant cap and matronly shawl. There is a tall brother strolling about the room, and a white-haired papa, opening his evening paper under the welcome blaze. Ellen's eyes would fain linger on the pleasant group, but the inexorable butler closes the shutters in her face.

One day Ellen was surprised by a visit from her friend Felicia

Rothwell. That young lady had not long since returned from Paris, and had traced Ellen from her Kensington lodging. Ellen described as shortly as possible her father's strange discovery. Felicia, not often excited, received the news very quietly. "I always thought you were a princess in disguise," she remarked. "Nice things suit you. That pretty dress is very becoming."

"My father likes to see me well dressed," Ellen said, "and he is very generous."

"You will give no more lessons in Spanish, Miss Waldron?"

"Not just now, whilst he is ill, but when he is well again, as many as you please. I like the work. What should I have done without you, Felicia?"

"True. You made me a very great service, did you not? Why did you not tell me you were so badly off?"

"Was I badly off?"

"I have heard nice stories from your landlady at Kensington."

"She was paid every farthing," said Ellen, flushing indignantly.

"It was not that. What did you mean by living entirely on dry bread and watered milk for a month? and all the while smiling at me as if everything was well with you – looking quietly at my new books and statuettes, and hearing how much money I had just flung away for them, and all the while ——"

"Bread and milk is excellent diet. Numbers of people live on it, and are strong and merry."

"It is not the sort of food for London."

"Well, don't let us talk any more of that time."

"Of the present, then. Will you come and stay with me at Amberwolds? It is a pretty country spot of mine, about ten miles from London. We are staying there now. Come."

"You forget. My father is ill."

"Afterwards then, as soon as he is well. In the meantime, what are you doing with yourself? You look worn-out. Have you books to read? Don't attempt anything more dry than a novel. Get some good novels."

"Recommend me a good one; I don't like filling my brain with rubbish. Name me one of a lofty spirit, eloquent, simple, and full of materials for pictures."

"At once. Read *Sunward*, by Arthur Ellis. You are smiling. You read it."

"Yes."

"What do you think of it?"

Ellen's eyes flashed and fell dreamy.

"I can scarcely tell you, because I cannot find words rich enough or delicate enough to clothe my meaning. I have made it a shrine. It is my friend. It will be to me a 'joy forever'."

"The world raves about it. What a thing it is to write a book like that, and become a hero. Have you seen the illustrated edition?"

"Yes; it is here."

"I want to hear you criticize the pictures."

"I also wish for your opinion of them. Let us get the book and look at them together."

"I tell you beforehand that I think them fine; but you are hard to please. Mr. Ellis is extremely well satisfied."

"Mr. Ellis! do you know him?"

"Yes, he is staying at Amberwolds just now. I suppose it is an honour having so great a lion under one's humble roof. But we met him abroad before the book came out."

"I am a hero-worshipper. Tell me what he is like."

"In person or in character?"

"Both; that I may know the whole."

"Oh, he is quite cut upon the hero pattern. He is very good-looking. You romancists look to that kind of thing. As to his character, I do not pretend to analyse it. By-and-by you must meet him at Amberwolds, and judge for yourself. But let us look at the pictures. Oh, see, if you want an idea of his physique, look here. This figure is very like him, especially the eyes and brow, and the attitude of the head. I had forgotten that. Several have remarked it."

Ellen started a little, then bent over the wood-cut, and smiling, said simply, —

"Indeed!"

"Well, it is not a good head?"

"Yes, it is a good head."

"How flushed you look! You are not well. I suppose you never go out – have been nowhere? By the way, were you at the Academy Exhibition this summer?"[11]

"Several times."

"There was a picture which we all thought very like you: John raved about it[12]. He wanted to buy it, but it was marked 'sold'."

Ellen grew hot at the mention of the name John.

"It is not much like me," she said quickly, "but it is a pretty good likeness of my mother. I painted it from the miniature in an old locket?"

"You painted it!"

"Yes; it is upstairs in the gallery."

"Well, you are an astonishing person. You have taken my breath away. I was just going to tell you that I heard it a good deal noticed. It has been called very clever."

"I am glad. We heard something of that kind before, and it pleased my father."

"Let me see what other wonders you have been achieving. Fetch me your portfolio."

Ellen brought it to her, forgetting quite about certain rough sketches which she had left in it. On one of these Felicia soon pounced.

"Why, what is this? have you been copying one of those woodcuts? but no, this is more like the rough draught of a first idea than an important copy!"

Ellen blushed, she scarcely knew why, but she replied coolly,

---

11. The annual summer exhibition of the work of many living artists at the Royal Academy in London.
12. Felicia's brother.

"Yes, it is a first sketch. I made a great many before I could feel moderately satisfied."

Felicia regarded her in perplexities.

"Do you mean," she said at last, "that you illustrated that book?"

Ellen nodded her head.

"You are the oddest creature I ever knew! Not that I am surprised at your success. I always knew what you could do. But you are so slow to mention it, and you seem so little elated."

"I am very glad, but I am afraid I grow more and more unlike your ideal woman, wholly wrapt up in, and soul-satisfied with, a grand intellectual pursuit."

"You are not going to prove an ungrateful renegade?"

"No; I love Art. I will be faithful to her. She shall get my life's happiness into her keeping. But somehow she is not so often first as she used to be. For a time I had almost forgotten my meaner tastes, my housekeeping, and my nurse-tending. Caring for my father has brought them back upon me, I think. Somehow I feel that Art will not saturate my life with contentment, as I once dreamed she could do."

Felicia glanced up in Ellen's eyes, wide open and absent for the moment, and then glanced down again at the sketch, saying nothing. The sarcastic reply was not ready as usual. Her next remark changed the conversation. She said, —

"Let me tell you that you have got that likeness even more remarkable in this rough drawing than in the finished engraving."

Ellen replied, smiling, —

"That is singular, since I have never seen the person in question."

"It must have been an inspiration."

And after this Felicia suddenly said good-by, and went away.

2

'The Hungry Death.'
All the Year Round. 1880.

Introduction

Inishbofin (spelled Innisbofin in the story), whose name means island of the white cow, is an island off the coast of Connemara in the west of Ireland. The timing of the famine described in Mulholland's story is not specified, though the narrative makes it clear that it took place in the recent past. In fact there was a severe local famine on Innisbofin in the winter of 1872–3, a few years before the story was published in 1880. Undoubtedly, though, stories of the Irish Great Famine of the 1840s may have also informed the narrative.

The story concerns the resentment of relatively well-off but emotionally awkward Brigid Lavelle against Coll Prendergast, the man she loves, when he takes up with a poorer woman, Moya Maillie. It leads her, initially, to deny them food during the famine but in a redemptive gesture she herself dies in providing it to them. The story of an island woman in a troubled relationship is an obvious anticipation of Emily Lawless's *Grania* (1892), though this story is a religious morality tale about the necessity of forgiveness. Yeats had republished 'The Hungry Death' in *Representative Irish Tales*, the year before the Lawless novel was published. Critical interest in "The Hungry Death" has focused on its depiction of famine.

I

It had been a wild night in Innisbofin, an Irish island perched far out among Atlantic breakers, as the bird flies to Newfoundland. Whoever has weathered an ocean hurricane will have some idea of the fury with which the tempest assaults and afflicts such lonely rocks. The creatures who live upon them, at the mercy of the winds and waves, build their cabins low, and put stones on the roof to keep the thatch from flying off on the trail of Mother Carey's chickens;[1] and having made the sign of the cross over their threshold at night, they sleep soundly, undisturbed by the weird and appalling voices which have sung alike the lullaby and death-keen of all their race.[2] In winter, rain or storm is welcome to rage round them, even though fish be frightened away, and food be scarce, but when wild weather encroaches too far upon the spring, then threats of the "hungry death" are heard with fear in its mutterings.

Is anyone to blame for this state of things? The people have a good landlord; but the greater part of the island is barren bog and rock. No shrub will grow upon it, and so fiercely is it swept by storm that the land by the northern and eastern coasts is only a picturesque wilderness, all life sheltering itself in three little thatched villages to the south. The sea is the treasury of the inhabitants, and no more daring hearts exist than those that fight these waves, often finding death in their jaws; but a want of even the rudest piers as defence against the Atlantic makes the seeking of bread upon the waters a perilous, and often an entirely impossible, exploit.

Bofin is of no mean size, and has a large population. Light hearted and frugal, the people feel themselves a little nation, and will point out to you with pride the storied interest of their island. In early ages it was a seat of learning, witness the ruins of St.

---

1. A folk name for the European Storm Petrel indicative of its reputation for ill fortune.
2. Keening is a traditional form of vocal lament for the dead.

Coleman's school and church;[3] in Elizabeth's day[4] the handsome masculine queen, Grace O'Malley,[5] built herself a fort on a knoll facing the glories of the western sky; and on the straggling rocks which form the harbour Cromwell raised those blackened walls, still welded into the rock and fronting the foam.[6] The island has a church, a school, a store where meal, oil, soap, ropes, etc., can be had, except when contrary winds detain the hooker which plies to and from Galway with such necessaries.[7]

Foreign sailors, weather-bound in Bofin, are welcomed, and invited to make merry. Pipers and fiddlers come and go, and when times are good are kept busy making music for dancing feet. Even when the wolf is within a pace of the door laughter and song will ring about his ears, so long as the monster can be beaten back by one neighbour from another neighbour's threshold. But there comes a day when he enters where he will, and the bones of the people are his prey. Last night's was a spring storm, and many a 'Lord have mercy on us!' went up in the silent hours, as the flooding rain that unearths the seedlings was heard seething on the wind; yet Bofin wakened out of its nightmare of terror green and gay, birds carolling in a blue sky, and the ring of the boat-maker's hammer suggesting peace and prosperity. Through the dazzling sunshine a girl came rowing herself in a small boat that darted rapidly along the water. The oars made a quick, pleasant thud on the air, the larks sang in the clouds, and the girl poured out snatches of a song of her own in a plaintive and mellow voice. The tune was wild and mournful; the Irish words of the ever-recurring refrain might be freely translated thus:

---

3. A ruined medieval abbey on the island.
4. Elizabeth Tudor (1533–1603), Queen of England and Ireland.
5. Grace O'Malley (1503–1603) was a Gaelic ruler in Connaught who was sometimes known as the 'pirate queen.' She built a stronghold on the island.
6. Oliver Cromwell (1599–1658), English Puritan military leader, had a fort built on the island for the detention of Catholic clergy.
7. A hooker is a small sailing vessel used off the coast of the west of Ireland.

Fearful was her wooing,
  Ululu!
All her life undoing.
  Ululu!

When his face she sighted,
Back she fell affrighted,
Death and she were plighted,
  Ululu!

A strange song for such a gay, glittering morning! Thud, thud, went the oars, and the girl's kerchief fell back from her head as the firm elastic figure swayed with the wholesome exercise.

Never was a fairer picture of health, strength, and beauty. Her thick, dark-red hair filled with the sunshine as a sponge fills with water; her red-brown eyes seemed to emit sparks of fire as the shadows deepened round them in the strong light. Two little round dimples fixed at the corners of the proud curved mouth whispered a tale of unusual determination lying at the bottom of a passionate nature. There was nothing to account for her curious choice of a song this brilliant morning, except the love of dramatic contrasts that exists in some eager souls. Suddenly she shipped her oars, and sat listening to the waves lapping the edges of the seaweed-fringed cliffs. 'I thought I heard someone calling me,' she muttered, looking up and down with a slight shudder but a bold gaze—'Brigid, Brigid, Brigid!' then, with a little laugh, she dipped her oars again, burst into a lively song, so reeling with merriment that it was wonderful how she found breath for it, and her boat flew along the glittering waves like a gull.

Above the broad, shelving, shingly beach within the harbour stood the school, the store, and some of the best dwellings on the island, and high and dry on the dreaming shingle the boat-maker was at work with a knot of gossips around him. The sky over their heads was a soft vivid blue; the brown-fringed rocks loomed against a sea almost too dazzling to look upon; the dewy green fields lay like scattered emeralds among the rocks and hollows.

"Lord, look to us!' said a man in a sou'-wester hat, "if the spring doesn't mend. Half my prates was washed clane out o' the ground last night."

"Whist, man, whist," said the boat-maker cheerfully. "Pick them up an' put them in again."

"Bedad," said an old fisherman, "the fish has got down to the bottom of all eternity. Ye might as well go fishin' for mermaids."

"Aren't yez ashamed to grumble," cried a hearty voice joining the group, "an' sich a mornin' as this? I tell ye last night was the last o' the rain."

"Ye have the hopes o' youth about ye, Coll Prendergast," said the old fisherman, looking at the strong frame and smiling bronzed face of the young man before him. "If yer words is not truth, it's the seaweed we'll be atin' afore next winther's out."

"Faix, some of it doesn't taste so bad," said Coll, laughing, "an' a little of it dried makes capital tabaccy. But whist! if here isn't Brigid Lavelle, come all the way from West Quarter in her pretty canoe."

The sound of oars had been heard coming steadily nearer, and suddenly Brigid's boat shot out from behind a mass of rock, making, with its occupant, such a picture on the glittering sea that the men involuntarily smiled as they shaded their eyes with their hands to look. Resting on her oars she smiled at them in return, while the sunshine gilded her perfect oval face, as brown as a berry, burnished the copper-hued hair rippling above her black, curved brows, and deepened the determined expression of her full red mouth. Her dress, the costume of the island, was only remarkable for the freshness and newness of its material—a deep crimson skirt of wool, with a light print bodice and short tunic, and a white kerchief thrown over the back of her head.

As she neared the shore Coll sprang into the water, drew her canoe close to the rocks, and, making it fast, helped her to land.

"That's a han'some pair," said the old fisherman to the boat-maker. "I hear their match is as good as made."

"Coll's in luck," said the other. "A rich beauty is not for ivery man."

"She's too proud, I'm thinking. Look at the airs of her now, an' him wet up to the knees in her sarvice."

"Yer mild, man, an' ye forgot yer coortin'. Let the crature toss her head while she can."

Brigid had proceeded to the store, where her purchases were soon made—a sack of meal, a can of oil, a little tea and sugar, and some white flour. The girl had a frown on her handsome brows as she did her business, and took but little notice of Coll, who busied himself gallantly with her packages. When all were stored in the boat, he handed her in, and stood looking at her, wondering if she would give him a smile in return for his attentions.

"Let me take the oars, Brigid. Ye'll be home in half the time."

"No, thank ye," she answered shortly. "I'll row my own boat as long as I can."

Coll smiled broadly, half amused and half admiring, and again sought for a friendly glance at parting, but in vain. The face that vanished out of his sight behind the cliff was cold and proud as though he had been her enemy. After he had turned and was striding up the beach the look that he had wanted to see followed him, shot through a rift in the rocks, where Brigid paused and peered with a tenderness in her eyes that altered her whole face. If Coll had seen that look this story might never have been written.

As the girl's boat sped past the cliffs towards home she frowned, thinking how awkward it was that she should have met Coll Prendergast on the beach. He must have known the errand that brought her to the store, and how dare he smile at her like that before he knew what answer she would give him? Coll's uncle and Brigid's father had planned a match between the young people, and the match-making was to be held that night at Brigid's father's house. Therefore had she come early in the morning in her boat to the store, to buy provisions for the evening's entertainment. Obedience to her father had obliged her to do this, but her own strong will revolted from the proceeding. She was proud, handsome, and an heiress, and did not like to be so easily won.

Brigid's father was sitting at the fire—a consumptive-looking man, with a wistful and restless eye.

"Father, I have brought very little flour. The hooker hasn't got in."

"Sorra wondher, an' sich storms. 'Tis late in the year for things to be this ways."

Brigid arranged her little purchases on the dresser and sat down at the table, but her breakfast—a few roasted potatoes and mug of buttermilk—remained untasted before her.

"Father, isn't you an' me happy as we are? Why need I marry in sich a hurry?"

"Because a lone woman's better with a husband, my girl."

"I'm not a lone woman. Haven't I got you?"

"Not for long, avourneen machree.[8] I'm readyin' to go this good while."

"But I will hold you back," cried Brigid, passionately, throwing her strong arms around his neck.

"You can't, asthoreen.[9] I'm wanted yonder, and it's time I was gettin' on with my purgatory.[10] An' there's bad times comin', an' I will not let you face them alone."

"I could pack up my bundles and be off to America," said Brigid, stoutly, dashing away tears.

"I will not have you wanderin' over the world like a stray bird," said the father, emphatically; and Brigid knew there was nothing more to be said.

---

8. An English version of a Gaelic term of endearment meaning, 'Oh, darling, my heart.'
9. An English version of a Gaelic term of endearment meaning, 'Oh, little love.'
10. A place or state where Christians believe that those who have died experience the temporal punishment due to sin before being admitted to heaven.

Lavelle's prosperity appeared before the world in a great deal of clean whitewash outside the house, and an interior more comfortable than is usual on the island. The cabin consisted of two rooms—the kitchen, with earthen floor and heather-lined roof, roosting-place for cocks and hens, and with its dresser, old and worm-eaten, showing a fair display of crockery; and the best room, containing a bed, a few pictures on sacred subjects, some sea-shells on the chimney-piece, an ornamental tray, an old gun, and an ancient, time-blackened crucifix against the wall, this last having been washed ashore one morning after the wreck of a Spanish ship. This was the finest house in Bofin, and Tim Lavelle, having returned from seeing the world and married late in life, had settled down in it, and on the most fertile bit of land on the island. It was thought he had a stockingful of money in the thatch, which would of course be the property of his daughter; so no wonder if the handsome Brigid has grown up a little spoiled with the knowledge of her own happy importance.

As she went about her affairs this morning she owned to herself that she would not be sorry to be forced to be Coll's wife in spite of her pride. True, he had paid her less court hitherto than any other young man on the island, and she longed to punish him for that; but what would become of her if she saw him married to another? Oh, if they had only left the matter to herself she could have managed it so much better—could have plagued him to her heart's content, and made him anxious to win her by means of the difficulties she would have thrown in his way. Had Coll been as poor as he seemed to be, with nothing but his boat and fishing-tackle, she would have been easier to woo, for then eagerness to bestow on him the contents of that stocking in the thatch would have swept away the stumbling-block of her pride. But his uncle had saved some money, which was to be given to Prendergast on the day of his marriage with her. It was a made-up match like Judy O'Flaherty's, while Brigid's proud head was crazed on the subject of being loved for her love's sake alone.

"I'll have to give him my hand tonight," she said, folding her brown arms, and standing straight in the middle of the room she had been dusting and decorating. "I be to obey father, an' I'll shame nobody afore the neighbours. But match-makin' isn't marryin'; and if it was to break my heart an' do my death I'll find means to plague him into lovin' me yet."

Having made this resolve, she let down her long hair, that looked dark bronze while she sat in the corner putting on her shoes, and turned to gold as she walked through a sunbeam crossing the floor, and having brushed it out and twisted it up again in a coil round her head, she finished her simple toilet and went out to the kitchen to receive her visitors.

The first that arrived was Judy O'Flaherty, an old woman with a smoke-dried face, who sat down in the chimney corner and lit her pipe. Judy was arrayed in a large patchwork quilt folded like a shawl, being too poor to indulge in the luxury of a cloak. But the quilt, made of red and white calico patches, was clean, and the cap on her head was fresh and neat.

"I give ye joy of Coll Prendergast," said Judy heartily. "Ye ought to be the glad girl to get sich a match."

"Why ought I be glad?" asked Brigid, angrily. "It's all as one may think."

"Holy Mother, girl! don't be sendin' them red sparks out o' yer eyes at me; Where d' ye see the likes o' Coll, I'm askin', with his six feet if he's an inch, an' his eyes like the blue on the Reek afore nightfall!"[11]

Brigid's heart leaped to hear him praised, and she turned away her face to hide the smile that curled her lips.

"An' yer match so aisy made for ye, without trouble to either o' ye. Not like some poor cratures, that have to round the world afore they can get one to put a roof over their heads or a bit in their mouths. It's me that knows. Sure wasn't I a wanderin' bein'

---

11. The Reek refers to Croagh Patrick, a pilgrimage mountain in Co. Mayo associated with St Patrick.

doin' day's works in the mountains, and as purty a girl as you, Miss Brigid, on'y I hadn't the stockin' in the thatch, nor the good father to be settlin' for me. An' sore and tired an' spent I was when one night I heard a knock at the door o' the house I was workin' in, an' a voice called out: 'Get up, Judy; here's a man come to marry you!' Maybe I didn't dress quick; an' who was there but a woman that knew my mother long ago, an' she had met a widow-man that wanted somebody to look after his childer. An' she brought him to me, an' wakened me out o' my sleep for fear he'd take the rue. An' we all sat o'r the fire for the rest o' the night to make the match, and in the first morning light we went down to Father Daly and got married. There's my marriage for ye, an' the rounds I had to get it, an' many a wan is like me. An' yet yer tossin' yer head at Coll, you that hasn't as much as the trouble o' bein' axed."

The smile had gone off Brigid's face. This freedom from trouble was the very thing that troubled her. She would rather have had the excitement of being "axed" a hundred questions. As they talked the sunshine vanished and the rain again fell in torrents. Brigid looked out of the door with a mischievous hope that the guests might be kept at home and the match-making postponed.

Judy rocked herself and groaned:

"Oh, musha, the pratees, the pratees! Oh, Lord, look down with mercy on the poor!" then suddenly became silent and began telling her beads.

A slight lull in the storm brought the company in a rush to the door, with bursts of laughter, groans for the rain and the potatoes, shaking and drying of cloaks and coats, and squealing and tuning up of pipes. Among the rest came Coll, smiling and confident as ever, with an arch look in his eyes when they met Brigid's, and not the least symptom of fear or anxiety in his face. Soon the door was barred against the storm, the fish-oil lamp lighted, laughter, song, and dancing filled the little house, and the rotting potatoes and the ruinous rains were forgotten as completely as though the Bofin population had been goddesses and gods, with whose nectar and ambrosia no such thing as weather could dare to interfere.

"Faith, ye must dance with me, Brigid," said Coll, after she had refused him half-a-dozen times.

"Why must I dance with you?"

"Oh, now, don't you know what's goin' on in there?" said Coll, roguishly, signing towards the room where father and uncle were arguing over money and land.

"I do," said Brigid, with all the red fire of her eyes blazing out upon him. "But, mind ye, this match-makin' is none o' my doin'."

"Why then, avourneen?"

"I'm not goin' to marry a man that on'y wants a wife, an' doesn't care a pin whether it's me or another."

"Bedad, I do care," said Coll, awkwardly. "I'm a bad hand at the speakin', but I care entirely."

But Brigid went off and danced with another man.

Coll was puzzled. He did not understand her the least. He was a simple straightforward fellow, and had truly been in love with Brigid—a fact which his confident manner had never allowed her to believe. Latterly he had begun to feel afraid of her; whenever he tried to say a tender word, that red light in her eyes would flash and strike him dumb. He had hoped that when their "match was made" she would have grown a little kinder; but it seemed she was only getting harsher instead. Well, he would try and hit on some way to please her; and, as he walked home that night, he pondered on all sorts of plans for softening her proud temper and satisfying her exacting mind.

On her side, Brigid saw that she had startled him out of his ordinary easy humour, and, congratulating herself on the spirit she had shown, resolved to continue her present style of proceeding. Not one smile would she give him, till she had, as she told herself, nearly tormented him to death. How close she was to keep to the letter of her resolution could not at this time be foreseen.

Every evening after this Coll travelled half the island to read some old treasured newspaper to the sickly Lavelle, and bringing various little offerings to his betrothed. Everything that Bofin could supply in the way of a love-gift was sought by him, and presented to her. Now it was a few handsome shells purchased from a foreign sailor in the harbour, or it was the model of a boat he had carved for her himself; and all this attention was not without its lasting effect. Unfortunately, however, while Brigid's heart grew more soft, her tongue only waxed more sharp, and her eyes more scornful. The more clearly she perceived that she would soon have to yield, the more haughty and capricious did she become. Had the young man been able to see behind outward appearances he would have been thoroughly satisfied, and a good deal startled at the vehemence of the devotion that had grown up and strengthened for him in that proud and wayward heart. As it was he felt more and more chilled by her continued coldness, and began to weary of a pursuit which seemed unlikely to be either for his dignity or his happiness.

Meanwhile the rain went on falling. The spring was bad, the summer was bad, potatoes were few and unwholesome, the turf lay undried and rotting on the bog. Distress began to pinch the cheerful faces of the islanders, and laughter and song were half-drowned in murmurs of fear. At the sight of so much sorrow and anxiety around her, Brigid's heart began to ache and to smite and reproach her for her selfish and unruly humours. One night, softened by the sufferings of others, she astonished herself by falling on her knees and giving humble thanks to heaven for the undeserved happiness that was awaiting her. She vowed that the next time Coll appeared she would put her hand in his, and let the love of her heart shine out in the smiles of her eyes. Had she kept this vow it might have been well with her, but her habit of vexing had grown all too strong to be cured in an hour. At the first sight of her lover's anxious face in the doorway all her passion for tormenting him returned.

It was an evening in the month of May; the day had been cold and wet, and as dark as January, but the rain had ceased, the clouds had parted, and one of those fiery sunsets burst upon the world that sometimes appear unexpectedly in the midst of stormy weather. In Bofin, where the sun drops down the heavens from burning cloud to cloud, and sinks in the ocean, the whole island was wrapped in a crimson flame. Brigid stood at her door, gazing at the wonderful spectacle of the heavens and sea, looking herself strangely handsome, with her bronze hair glittering in the ruddy sun light, and that dark shadow about her eyes and brows which, except when she smiled, always gave such a look of tragedy to her face. She was waiting for Coll, with softened lips and downcast eyes, and was so lost in her thoughts that she did not see him when he stood beside her.

He remained silently watching her for a few moments, thinking that if she would begin to look like that he would be ready to love her as well as he had ever loved her, and to forget that he had ever wearied of her harassing scorn. At this very moment Brigid was rehearsing within her mind a kind of little speech which was to establish a good understanding between them.

"I'm sorry I vexed you so often, for I love you true," were the words she had meant to speak; but suddenly seeing Coll by her side, the habitual taunt flew involuntarily to her lips.

"You here again!" she said disdainfully. "Then no one can say but you're the perseverinest man in the island!"

"Maybe I'm too perseverin'," said Coll, quietly, and, as Brigid looked at him with covert remorse, she saw something in his face that frightened her. His expression was a mixture of weariness and contempt. He was not hurt, or angry, or amused, as she had been accustomed to see him, but tired of her insolence, which was ceasing to give him pain. A sudden consciousness of this made Brigid turn sick at heart, and she felt that she had at last gone a little too far, that she had been losing him all this time while triumphantly thinking to win him. Oh, why could she not speak and say the word that she wanted to say? While this anguish came into her thoughts her brows grew darker than ever, and the warmth ebbed gradually out of her cheek. They went silently into the house, where Brigid took up her knitting, and Coll dropped into his seat beside Lavelle. The bad times, the rotting crops, the scant expectations of a harvest, were discussed by the two men while Brigid sat fighting with her pride, and trying to decide on what she ought to say or do. Before she had made up her mind, Coll had said good-evening abruptly, and gone out of the house.

The young fisherman's home was in Middle Quarter Village, a cluster of grey stone cabins close to the sea, and to reach it Coll had to cross almost the whole breadth of the island. He set out on his homeward walk with a weary and angry heart. Brigid's dark unyielding face followed him, and he was overwhelmed by a fit of unusual depression. He whistled as he went, trying to shake it off. Why should he fret about a woman who disliked him, and who probably loved another whom her father disapproved? Let her do what she liked with herself and her purse. Coll would persecute her no more.

The red light had slowly vanished off the island, and the dark cliffs on the oceanward coast loomed large and black against the still lurid sky. Deep drifts of brown and purple flecked with amber swept across the bogs, and filled up the dreary horrors of the barren and irreclaimable land which Coll had to traverse on his way to the foam-drenched village where the fishermen lived. The heavens cooled to paler tints, a ring of yellow light encircled the island with its creeping shadows and ghost-like rocks. Twilight was descending when Coll heard a faint cry from the distance, like the call of a belated bird or the wail of a child in distress.

At first he thought it was the wind or a plover, but straining his eyes in the direction whence it came he saw a small form standing solitary in the middle of a distant hollow, a piece of treacherous bog, dangerous in the crossing except to knowing feet. Hurrying to the spot he found himself just in time to succour a fellow-creature in distress.

Approaching as near as he could with ease to the person who

had summoned him, he saw a very young girl standing gazing towards him with piteous looks. She was small, slight, poorly and scantily clad, and carried a creel full of sea-rack[12] on her slight and bending shoulders. A pale after-gleam from the sky fell where she stood, young and forlorn, in the shadowy solitude, and lit up a face round and delicately pale, reminding one of a daisy; a wreath of wind-tossed yellow hair, and eyes as blue as forget-me-nots. Terror had taken possession of her, and she stretched out her hands appealingly to the strong man, who stood looking at her from the opposite side of the bog. Coll observed her in silence for a few moments. It seemed as if he had known her long ago, and that she belonged to him; yet if so, it was in another state of existence, for he assured himself that she was no one with whom he had any acquaintance. However that might be, he was determined to know more of her now, for, with her childlike, appealing eyes and outstretched hands, she went straight into Coll's heart, to nestle there like a dove of peace for evermore.

"Aisy, asthoreen," cried Coll across the bog, "I'm goin' to look after ye. Niver ye fear."

He crossed the morass with a few rapid springs, and stood by her side.

"Give me the creel, avourneen, till I land it for ye safe."

A few minutes and the burthen was deposited on the safe side of the bog, and then Coll came back and took the young girl in his arms

"Keep a good hoult round my neck, machree."

It was a nice feat for a man to pick his way through this bog, with even so small a woman as this in his arms. The girl clung to him in fear, as he swayed and balanced himself on one sure stone after another, slipping here and stumbling there, but always recovering himself before mischief could be done. At last the deed was accomplished—the goal was won.

---

12. 'A creel full of sea-rack' might be rendered as 'a basket full of seaweed.' 'Rack' is generally spelled 'wrack.'

"Ye were frightened, acushla," said Coll, tenderly.[13]

"I was feared of dhrownin' ye," said the girl, looking wistfully in his face with her great, blue eyes.

"Sorra matther if ye had," said Coll, laughingly, "except that maybe ye'd ha' been dhrowned too. Now, which ways are ye goin'? and maybe ye 'd be afther teilin' me who ye are?"

"I'm Moya Maillie," said the girl; "an' I live in Middle Quarter Village."

"Why, yer niver little Moya that I used to see playing round poor Maillie's door that's dead an' gone! And how did ye grow up that ways in a night?"

"Mother says I'll niver grow up," laughed Moya; "but I'm sixteen on May mornin', and I'll be contint to be as I am."

"Many a fine lady would give her fortune to be contint with that same," said Coll, striding along with the creel on his shoulders, and glancing down every minute at the sweet white-flower-like face that flitted through the twilight at his side. Thus Brigid's repentance would now come all too late, for Coll had fallen in love with little Moya.

How he brought her home that night to a bare and poverty-stricken cabin in the sea-washed fishing village, and restored her like a stray lamb to her mother, need not be told. Her mother was a widow and the mother of seven, and Moya's willing labour was a great part of the family support. She mended nets for the fishermen, and carried rack for the neighbour's land, knitted stockings to be sent out to the great world and sold, and did any other task which her slender and eager hands could find to do. Coll asked himself in amazement how it was that having known her as a baby he had never observed her existence since then. Now an angel, he believed, had led her out into the dreary bog to stand waiting for his sore heart on that blessed day of days. And he would never marry anyone but little Moya.

---

13. An English version of a Gaelic term of endearment meaning 'darling.'

It was impossible they could marry while times were so bad, but, every evening after this, Moya might be seen perched on an old boat upon the shingle, busy with her knitting—her tiny feet, bare and so brown, crossed under the folds of her old worn red petticoat, with a faint rose-pink in her pale cheeks, and a light of extraordinary happiness in her childlike blue eyes. Coll lay on the shingle at her feet, and these two found an Elysium in each other's company.[14] There was much idleness perforce for the men of Bofin at this time, and Coll filled up his hours looking after the concerns of the Widow Maillie, carrying Moya's burdens, and making the hard times as easy for her as he could. When people would look surprised at him and ask: "Arrah, thin, what about Brigid Lavelle?" Coll would answer: "Oh, she turned me off long ago. Everybody knows that she could not bear the sight of me."

In the meantime Brigid, at the other end of the island, was watching daily and hourly for Coll's reappearance. As evening after evening passed without bringing him, her heart misgave her more and more, and she mourned bitterly over her own harshness and pride. Oh, if he would only come again with that wistful, questioning look in his brave face, how kindly she would greet him, how eagerly put her hand in his grasp! As the rain rained on through the early summer evenings there would often come before sunset a lightening and a brightening all over the sky, and this was the hour at which Brigid used to look for her now ever-absent lover. Climbing to the top of the hill, she would peer over the sea-bounded landscape, with its dark stretches of bog, and strips and flecks of green, towards the grey irregular line of the fishing village, the smoke of which she could see hanging against the horizon. Her face grew paler and her eyes dull, but to no one, not even to her father, would she admit that she was pining for Coll's return. She had always lived much by herself, and had few gossiping friends to bring her news. At last, unable to bear the

---

14. Elysium is a paradise for the dead in ancient Greek religion.

suspense any longer, she made an excuse of business at the store on the beach; and before she had gone far among the houses of that metropolis of the island, she was enlightened as to the cause of her lover's defection.

"So ye cast him off. So ye giv' him to little Moya Maillie," were the words that greeted her wherever she turned. She smiled and nodded her head, as if heartily assenting to what was said, and content with the existing state of things; but as she walked away out of the reach of observing eyes, her face grew dark and her heart throbbed like to burst in her bosom. Almost mechanically she took her way home through the Middle Quarter Village, with a vague desire to see what was to be seen, and to hear whatever was to be heard. She passed among the houses without observing anything that interested her, but, as she left the village, by the seashore she came upon Coll and Moya sitting on a rock in the yellow light of a watery sunset, with a mist of sea-foam around them, and a net over their knees which they were mending between them. Their heads were close together, and Coll was looking in her face with the very look which, all these tedious days and nights, Brigid had been wearying to meet. She walked up beside them, and stood looking at them silently with a light in her eyes that was not good to behold.

"Brigid," said Coll, when he could bear it no longer, "for heaven's sake, are ye not satisfied yet?"

She turned from him, and fixed her strange glance on Moya.

"It was me before, an' it's you now," she said shortly. "He's a constant lover, isn't he?"

"I loved ye true, and ye scoffed and scorned me," said Coll, gently, as the gleam of anguish and despair in her eyes startled him. "I wasn't good enough for Brigid, but I'm good enough for Moya. We're neither of us as rich nor as clever as you, but we'll do for one another well enough."

Brigid laughed a sharp, sudden laugh, and still looked at Moya.

"For heaven's sake, take that wicked look off her face," cried

Coll, hastily. "What somdever way it is betune us three is yer own doin'; an', whether ye like it or not, it cannot now be helped."

"I will never forgive either of you," said Brigid, in a low, hard voice; and then, turning abruptly away, she set out on her homeward walk through the gathering shadows.

II

All through that summer the rain fell, and, when autumn came in Bofin, there was no harvest either of fuel or of food. The potato-seed had been for the most part washed out of the earth without putting forth a shoot, while those that remained in the ground were nearly all rotted by a loathsome disease. The smiling little fields that grew the food were turned into blackened pits, giving forth a horrid stench. Winter was beginning again, the year having been but one long winter, with seas too wild to be often braved by even the sturdiest of the fishermen, and the fish seeming to have deserted the island. Accustomed to exist on what would satisfy no other race, and to trust cheerfully to Providence to send them that little out of the earth and out of the sea, the people bore up cheerfully for a long time, living on a mess of Indian-meal once a day, mingled with such edible seaweed as they could gather off the rocks.[15] So long as shopkeepers in Galway and other towns could afford to give credit to the island, the hooker kept bringing such scanty supplies as were now the sole sustenance of the impoverished population. But credit began to fail, and universal distress on the mainland gave back an answering wail to the hunger-cry of the Bofiners. It is hard for anyone who has never witnessed such a state of things to imagine the condition of ten or twelve hundred living creatures on a barren island girded round with angry breakers; the strong arms around them paralyzed, first by the storms that dash their boats to pieces, and rend and destroy their fishing gear,

---

15. Indian meal, also referred to in the text as relief meal and yellow meal, was imported American maize that was sometimes used in Ireland during times of food shortage.

and the devastation of the earth that makes labour useless, and later by the faintness and sickness which comes from hunger long endured, and the cold from which they have no longer a defence. Accustomed as they are to the hardships of recurring years of trial, the Bofiners became gradually aware that a visitation was at hand for which there had seldom been a parallel. Earth and sea alike barren and pitiless to their needs, whence could deliverance come unless the heavens rained down manna into their mouths?

Alas! no miracle was wrought, and after a term of brave struggle, hope in Providence, cheerful pushing off of the terrible fears for the worst—after this, laughter, music, song faded out of the island; feet that had danced as long as it was possible now might hardly walk, and the weakest among the people began to die. Troops of children that a few months ago were rosy and sturdy, sporting on the sea-shore, now stretched their emaciated limbs by the fireless hearths, and wasted to death before their maddened mothers' eyes. The old and ailing vanished like flax before a flame. Digging of graves was soon the chief labour of the island, and a day seemed near at hand when the survivors would no longer have strength to perform even this last service for the dead.

Lavelle and his daughter were among the last to suffer from the hard times, and they shared what they had with their poor neighbours; but in course of time the father caught the fever which famine had brought in its train, and was quickly swept into his grave, while the girl was left alone in possession of their little property, with her stocking in the thatch and her small flock of "beasts" in the field. Her first independent act was to despatch all the money she had left by a trusty hand to Galway to buy meal, in one of those pauses in the bad weather which sometimes allowed a boat to put off from the island. The meal arrived after long, unavoidable delay, and Brigid became a benefactor to numbers of her fellow-creatures. Late and early she trudged from village to village and from house to house, doling out her meal to make it go as far as possible, till her own face grew pale and her step slow, for she stinted her own food to have the more to give away. Her "beasts" grew lean and dejected. Why should she feed them at the expense of human life? They were killed, and the meat given to her famishing friends. The little property of the few other well-to-do families in like manner melted away, and it seemed likely that "rich" and poor would soon all be buried in one grave.

In the Widow Maillie's house the famine had been early at work. Five of Moya's little sisters and brothers had one by one sickened and dropped upon the cabin floor. The two elder boys still walked about looking like galvanized skeletons, and the mother crept from wall to wall of her house trying to pretend that she did not suffer, and to cook the mess of rank-looking sea-weed, which was all they could procure in the shape of food. Coll risked his life day after day trying to catch fish to relieve their hunger, but scant and few were the meals that all his efforts could procure from the sea. White and gaunt he followed little Moya's steps, as with the spirit of a giant she kept on toiling among the rocks for such weeds or shell-fish as could be supposed to be edible. When she fell Coll bore her up, but the once powerful man was not able to carry her now. Her lovely little face was hollow and pinched, the cheek-bones cutting through the skin. Her sweet blue eyes were sunken and dim, her pretty mouth purple and strained. Her beauty and his strength were alike gone.

Three of the boys died in one night, and it took Coll, wasted as he was, two days to dig a grave deep enough to bury them. Before that week was over all the children were dead of starvation, and the mother scarcely alive. One evening Coll made his way slowly across the island from the beach, carrying a small bag of meal which he had unexpectedly obtained. Now and again his limbs failed, and he had to lie down and rest upon the ground; but with long perseverance and unconquerable energy he reached the little fishing village at last. As he passed the first house, Brigid Lavelle, pallid and worn, the spectre of herself, came out of the door with an empty basket. Coll and she stared at each other in melancholy amazement. It was the first time they had met since the memorable scene on the rocks many months ago, for Coll's entire time had been devoted to the Maillies, and Brigid had persistently kept out of his way, striving, by charity to others, to quench the fire of angry despair in her heart. Coll would scarcely have recognized her in her present death-like guise, had it not been for the still living glory of her hair.

The sight of Coll's great frame, once so stalwart and erect, now stooping and attenuated, his lustreless eyes, and blue, cold lips, struck horror into Brigid's heart. She utttered a faint, sharp cry and disappeared. Coll scarcely noticed her, his thoughts were so filled with another; and a little further on he met Moya coming to meet him, walking with a slow, uneven step that told of the whirling of the exhausted brain. Half blind with weakness she stretched her hands before her as she walked.

"The hungry death is on my mother at last. Oh, Coll, come in and see the last o' her!"

"Whist, machree! Look at the beautiful taste o' male I am bringin' her. Hard work I had to carry it from the beach, for the eyes o' the cretures is like wolves' eyes, an' I thought the longin' o' them would have dragged it out o' my hands. An', Moya, there's help comin' from God to us. There's kind people out in the world that's thinkin' o' our needs. The man that has just landed with a sack, an' giv' me this, says there's a hooker full o' male on its road to us this day. May the great Lord send us weather to bring it here."

"I'm 'feared—I'm 'feared it's too late for her," sobbed Moya, clinging to him.

They entered the cabin where the woman lay, a mere skeleton covered with skin, with the life still flickering in her glassy eyes. Coll put a little of the meal, as it was, between her lips, while Moya hastened to cook the rest on a fire made of the dried roots of heather. The mother turned loving looks from one to the other, tried to swallow a little of the food to please them, gasped, shuddered a little, and was dead.

It was a long, hard task for Coll and Moya to bury her, and when this was done they sat on the heather clasping each other's wasted hands. The sky was dark; the storm was coming on again. As night approached a tempest was let loose upon the island, and many famishing hearts that had throbbed with a little hope at the news of the relief that was on its way to them, now groaned, sickened, and broke in despair. Louder howled the wind, and the sea raged around the dangerous rocks towards which no vessel could dare to approach. It was the doing of the Most High, said the perishing creatures. His scourge was in His hand. Might His ever blessed will be done!

That evening Moya became delirious, and Coll watched all night by her side. At morning light he fled out and went round the village, crying out desperately to God and man to send him a morsel of food to save the life of his young love. The suffering neighbours turned pitying eyes upon him.

"I'm 'feared it's all over with her when she can't taste the say-weed any more," said one.

"Why don't ye go to Brigid Lavelle?" said another. "She hasn't much left, poor girl; but maybe she'd have a mouthful for you."

Till this moment Coll had felt that he could not go begging of Brigid; but, now that Moya's precious life was slipping rapidly out of his hands, he would suffer the deepest humiliation she could heap upon him, if only she would give him so much food as would keep breath in Moya's body till such time as, by Heaven's mercy, the storm might abate, and the hooker with the relief-meal arrive.

Brigid was alone in her house. A little porridge for some poor creature simmered on a scanty fire, and the girl stood in the middle of the floor, her hands wrung together above her head, and her brain distracted with the remembrance of Coll as she had seen him stricken by the scourge. All these months she had told her jealous heart that the Maillies were safe enough since they had Coll to take care of them. So long as there was a fish in the sea he would not let them starve, neither need he be in any danger himself. And so she had never asked a question about him or them. Now the horror of his altered face haunted her. She had walked through the direst scenes with courageous calm, but this one unexpected sight of woe had nearly maddened her.

A knock came to the door which at first she could not hear for the howling of the wind; but when she heard and opened there was Coll standing before her.

"Meal," he said faintly—"a little meal, for the love of Christ! Moya is dying."

A spasm of anguish and tenderness had crossed Brigid's face at the first words; but at the mention of Moya her face darkened.

"Why should I give to you or Moya?" she said coldly. "There's them that needs that help as much as ye."

"But not more," pleaded Coll. "Oh, Brigid, I'm not askin' for myself. I fear I vexed ye, though I did not mean it. But Moya niver did any one any harm. Will you give me a morsel to save her from the hungry death?"

"I said I niver would forgive either o' ye, an' I niver will," said Brigid, slowly. "Ye broke my heart, an' why wouldn't I break yours?"

"Brigid, perhaps neither you nor me has much longer to live. Will ye go before yer Judge with sich black words on yer lips?"

"That's my affair," she answered in the same hard voice, and then suddenly turning from him, shut the door in his face.

She stood listening within, expecting to hear him returning to implore her, but no further sound was heard; and, when she found he was gone, she dropped upon the floor with a shriek, and rocked herself in a frenzy of remorse for her wickedness.

"But I cannot help everyone," she moaned; "I'm starving myself, an' there's nothin' but a han'ful o' male at the bottom o' the bag."

After a while she got up, and carried the mess of porridge to the house for which she had intended it, and all that day she went about, doing what charity she could, and not tasting anything herself. Returning, she lay down on the heather, overcome with weakness, fell asleep, and had a terrible dream. She saw herself dead and judged; a black-winged angel put the mark of Cain on her forehead, and at the same moment Coll and Moya went, glorified and happy, hand in hand into heaven before her eyes. "Depart from me, you accursed," thundered in her ears; and she started wide awake to hear the winds and waves roaring unabated round her head.

Wet and shivering she struggled to regain her feet, and stood irresolute where to go. Dreading to return to her desolate home, she mechanically set her face towards the little church on the cliff above the beach. On her way to it she passed prostrate forms, dying or dead, on the heather, on the roadside, and against the cabin wails. A few weakly creatures, digging graves, begged from her as she went past, but she took no notice of anything, living or dead, making straight for the church. No one was there, and the storm howled dismally through the empty, barn-like building. Four bare, white-washed walls, and a rude wooden altar, with a painted tabernacle and cross—this was the church. On one long wall was hung a large crucifix, a white, thorn-crowned figure upon stakes of black-painted wood, which had been placed there in memory of a "mission" lately preached on the island; and on this Brigid's burning eyes fixed themselves with an agony of meaning. Slowly approaching it she knelt and stretched out her arms, uttering no prayer, but swaying herself monotonously to and fro. After a while the frenzied pain of remorse was dulled by physical exhaustion, and a stupor was stealing over her senses when a step entering the church startled her back into consciousness. Looking round she saw that the priest of the island had come in, and was wearily dragging himself towards the altar.

Father John was suffering and dying with his people. He had just now returned from a round of visits among the sick, during which he had sped some departing souls on their journey, and given the last consolation of religion to the dying. His own gaunt face and form bore witness to the unselfishness which had made all his little worldly goods the common property of the famishing.

Before he had reached the rails of the altar Brigid had thrown herself on her face at his feet.

"Save me, father, save me!" she wailed. "The sin of murther is on my soul!"

"Nonsense, child! No such thing. It is too much that you have been doing, my poor Brigid! I fear the fever has crazed your brain."

"Listen to me, father. Moya is dying, an' there is still a couple o' han'fuls o' male in the bag. Coll came an' asked me for her, an' I hated her because he left me, and I would not give it to him, an' maybe she is dead."

"You refused her because you hated her?" said the priest. "God help you, my poor Brigid. 'Tis true you can't save every life; but you must try and save this one."

Brigid gazed up at him, brightly at first, as if an angel had spoken, and then the dark shadow fell again into her eyes.

The priest saw it.

"Look there, my poor soul," he said, extending a thin hand towards the figure on the cross. "Did He forgive His enemies, or did He not?"

Brigid turned her fascinated gaze to the crucifix, fixed them on the thorn-crowned face, and, uttering a wild cry, got up and tottered out of the church.

Spurred by terror lest her amend should come too late, and Moya be dead before she could reach her, she toiled across the heather once more, over the dreary bogs, and through the howling storm. Dews of suffering and exhaustion were on her brow as she carefully emptied all the meal that was left of her store into a vessel, and stood for a moment looking at it in her hand.

"There isn't enough for all of us," she said, "an' some of us be to die. It was always her or me, her or me; an' now it'll be me. May Christ receive me, Moya, as I forgive you." And then she kissed the vessel and put it under her cloak.

Leaving the house, she was careless to close the door behind her, feeling certain that she should never cross the threshold again, and straining all her remaining strength to the task, she urged her lagging feet by the shortest way to the Middle Quarter Village. Dire were the sights she had to pass upon her way. Many a skeleton hand was outstretched for the food she carried; but Brigid was now deaf and blind to all appeals. She saw only Coll's accusing face, and Moya's glazing eyes staring terribly at her out of the rain-clouds. Reaching the Maillies' cabin, she found the door fastened against the storm.

Coll was kneeling in despair by Moya, when a knocking at the door aroused him. The poor fellow had prayed so passionately, and was in so exalted a state, that he almost expected to see an angel of light upon the threshold bring the food he had so urgently asked for. The priest had been there and was gone, the neighbours were sunk in their own misery; why should anyone come knocking like that, unless it were an angel bringing help? Trembling, he opened the door; and there was Brigid, or her ghost.

"Am I in time?" gasped she, as she put the vessel of food in his hand.

"Aye," said Coll, seizing it. In his transport of delight he would have gone on his knees and kissed her feet; but before he could speak, she was gone.

Whither should she go now? was Brigid's thought. No use returning to the desolate and lonesome home where neither food nor fire was any longer to be found. She dreaded dying on her own hearthstone alone, and faint as she was she knew what was now before her. Gaining the path to the beach, she made a last pull on her energies to reach the whitewashed walls, above which her fading eyes just dimly discerned the cross. The only face she now wanted to look upon again was that thorn-crowned face which was waiting for her in the loneliness of the empty and wind-swept church. Falling, fainting, dragging herself on again, she crept within the shelter of the walls. A little more effort, and she would be at His feet. The struggle was made, blindly, slowly, desperately, with a last rally of all the passion of a most impassioned nature; and at last she lay her length on the earthen floor under the cross. Darkness, silence, peace, settled down upon her. The storm raved around, the night came on, and when the morning broke, Brigid was dead.

III

Mildly and serenely that day had dawned, a pitiful sky looked down on the calamities of Bofin, and the vessel with the relief-meal sailed into the harbour. For many even then alive, the food came all too late, but to numbers it brought assuagement and salvation. The charity of the world was at work, and though much had yet to be suffered, yet the hungry death had been mercifully stayed. Thanks to the timely help, Moya lived for better times, and when her health was somewhat restored, she emigrated with Coll to America. Every night in their distant backwoods hut they pray together for the soul of Brigid Lavelle, who, when in this world, had loved one of them too well, and died to save the life of the other.

3

From *Marcella Grace*.
London, Kegan, Paul and Trench, 1886.

Chapters Eleven to Thirteen

Introduction

Marcella Grace grows up in the Liberties of Dublin with her father, a weaver. Her mother had been a lady. Mrs. O'Kelly, a Catholic landowner who lives in Merrion Square has a discussion with Father Daly, parish priest of Ballydownvalley, Distresna, Back o' the Mountains in Connaught where her Crane's Castle estate is situated and which she is afraid to visit because of growing violent attacks against landlords. She does not approve of her putative heirs, the O'Flahertys of Mount Ramshackle, who are deemed rack-renters because of the high rents they charge. However, she leaves her estate to Marcella whom she discovers to be her niece. One night in Dublin Marcella had helped a fugitive, suspected of murder, to evade capture from the police. He turns out to be Bryan Kilmartin of Inisheen, member of a landlord family near the O'Kelly estate, who had become involved with an agrarian group who are labelled as Fenians, though he had also tried to leave them. Marcella, having adopted O'Kelly as a surname, goes to stay with the Bryan Kilmartin and his mother before she is introduced to her new tenants, though Bryan fails to recognize her. Chapters eleven to thirteen, below, recount that stay, how Marcella gets to know the tenantry, without them knowing who she really is, and how she introduces herself to them as their new landlord with a show of kindness that bodes well for the future. As a Catholic she has the advantage of the guidance of the parish priest as she learns to care for the people. With Kilmartin she debates the land situation. She favours the continuance of landlordism whereas he does not. As in *Dunmara* on the question of women's professions, Mulholland allows for a debate between various views, though in both instances obviously favouring the more conservative position.

During the course of the rest of the novel, Bryan and Marcella fall in love and he is arrested for the murder in Dublin. At this point she tells him of their previous connection though he forbids her from perjuring herself at his trial in order to provide him with an alibi. He is convicted and sentenced to death, though this is commuted to life imprisonment. Marcella is subject to an assassination plot which is only frustrated by her potential assassin falling ill. She nurses the individual and in gratitude he confesses to the murder, enabling Bryan's release.

Agrarian violence in nineteenth-century Ireland was very often directed against landlords by tenants, often disgruntled with the level of their rents. An agricultural depression in the late 1870s led to the formation of the Irish National Land League which organized for the rights of tenants, resulting in various parliamentary land acts that increased the rights of tenants and ultimately paved the way for tenants to become owners of their farms. However, the Land League's agitation was often accompanied by agrarian violence, including assassination, against landlords and their agents, though it was not necessarily the cause of such violence. The most notorious killing was that of Lord Mountmorres in 1880. In *Marcella Grace* this violence is somewhat anomalously associated with the Fenians, a more urban, secret society, dedicated to political revolution, whose heyday had been the 1860s. Mainstream Fenianism had foresworn violent revolution by the 1880s, though various, small, related groups, often with American links, were involved in violent campaigns, such as the dynamite attacks in Britain in the 1880s. Agrarian violence was, nonetheless, often associated with Fenianism in Britain, including in the popular press. Hence perhaps Mulholland's decision to include the Fenians in *Marcella Grace*.

Another feature of the 1880s was attention to cases that were thought to be miscarriages of justice. The most famous case was that of Myles Joyce who was executed for murder in 1882, though he was widely believed to be innocent. That same year a man called Bryan Kilmartin was sentenced to life imprisonment for shooting and wounding a landlord's bailiff on Inishmore in the Aran Islands. But when another man confessed to the crime on his deathbed and when his wife appealed to the lord lieutenant an investigation was launched and he was released. The fact that the principal character in Mulholland's novel has the same name and finds himself in a similar predicament must be more than coincidence. Mulholland may thus be presumed to be making a case for having continuing faith in the justice system. Finally, like many other land war novels, many of whose authors were women, *Marcella Grace* features an empowered role for a woman, though by the end of the novel Marcella retreats somewhat into the shadow of her released husband.

CHAPTER ELEVEN
INISHEEN

The interior of the home at Inisheen (the little Isle), consisted of a few rooms and passages all on the same floor. The outer walls were of a great thickness, the chimneys stout and low, the windows small and square, the porch strong as a little tower, having two doors, one on each side, to be opened or shut in turn as the wind shifted. Set as it was in the middle of the wind-haunted lake, it had the look of a little fortress, and such it was to the inhabitants when they stood siege in it against the wintry elements. The three or four acres of green turf which surrounded the dwelling and sloped towards the rocks were studded with clumps of low growing trees and bushes, and a thick mat of ivy clung to every wall of the house from base to eaves. A varieties of sea-birds, gulls, puffins, curlews, and wild geese, made their nests in the rocks, or came in long flights from the sea, which, though invisible from Inisheen, was not far away and their shrill cries and pipings as they swept the lake like trails of mist gave notice when there was a storm at hand.

There were only two living-rooms at Inisheen, and the drawing room walls were two-thirds lined with books, the shelves for which had been set up by Bryan himself, when stress of circumstance drove him, with his mother, to put into the little island as a harbour. A few eastern rugs on the floor, some material of the same kind draping the short, deep-seated windows, with a pretty supply of foreign ornaments and curiosities, gave elegance and colour to the little interior, where fire as well as lamps burned on that summer night as a protection from chills and damps which, dropping down from the mountains and exhaling from the lake, might be seen any time from dark till dawn floating like wraiths upon the bosom of the waters. A harp stood in one corner of the room, and among the few pictures which the bookshelves had left space for on the walls were an engraving of Robert Emmett, speaking in his own defence upon his trial, and another of the old Irish House of Commons, containing a multitude of small figures, many of which were portraits.[1]

Marcella was sitting at a table, turning over some precious etchings; Mrs. Kilmartin was reclining on her couch, her eyes eagerly following the movements of her son, who walked about the room while the conversation turned on the future treatment of the discontented tenantry of Distresna.

---

1. Robert Emmet (1778–1803) led a brief insurrection for which he was executed. Before 1801 Ireland had a separate parliament that had two chambers, the houses of Commons and Lords. It was housed in a building in College Green, Dublin, which later became the Bank of Ireland.

Mrs. Kilmartin was a small, slight woman, looking more like a withered child than a woman who had matured and grown old. She was all white from head to foot except for her blue eyes and pink lips. Her hair was snow-white and dressed prettily on the top of her head, her face was delicately pale, and her gown and shawl were both of some soft white woollen material.

"We are not responsible for bringing her here, Bryan. Mrs. O'Kelly confided her to Father Daly, and Father Daly carried her off here at once to me. We have laid no plot to influence her movements. She is twenty-one years of age and capable of managing her own affairs. And indeed she has shown aptitude for the business and some originality in striking out a course for herself. My dear, will you tell Bryan what you have already been about?"

Marcella put aside the etchings, and leaning her elbows on the table, and clasping her hands under her chin, looked towards Bryan with a frank smile. She felt instinctively that he was less likely to identify her with the Liberties girl, so long as she smiled, for she had observed that it was generally when she looked grave or sad that he turned those puzzled inquiring glances on her which conveyed to her keen apprehension that the scene of his introduction to the secret closet was present to his mind. On that eventful night of his concealment, Marcella had certainly not smiled at him. A patient courage, an uncomplaining mournfulness had been expressed then by the eyes and lips which were irradiated now with a steady gladness which was by no means assumed. For, still lost as she was in delighted surprise at the change of fortune that had transferred her to this peaceful, refined, and romantic home, and placed her as a centre of interest between her hero and his mother, smiles came to her more naturally than they had ever done before in the course of her short life.

"I have been visiting my people with Father Daly," she said, "not however, as their landlord, but only as a friend of his. I begged him to let me make their acquaintance first and try to gain their good will before announcing myself as the future receiver of their rents."

"A happy thought," said Bryan, watching eagerly all the changes of her animated face. "And how have you found them?"

"I have only visited a few as yet. Father Daly is to come for me to-morrow again. In some of the cabins the people were as sullen and reserved as they looked hungry and poverty-stricken. In other places I thought them too civil. They seemed to distrust a stranger, even though she accompanied Father Daly. But in several cases I think I made my way as a friend. Miss O'Flaherty had told me that unless I gave them presents and made them great promises they would hate me. I gave them nothing and promised them nothing, yet, I think, I shall be welcome to some of them when I go back again."

"I do not doubt it. The freemasonry of human sympathy is hardly known to Miss Julia O'Flaherty. It is only too well understood by our poor Irish cottiers. I am glad you have made so good a beginning, Miss O'Kelly. That you should understand the people you have to deal with by personal experience rather than take them for granted through the counsels and representation of others is just what is most desirable for you. It is better for you to follow neither in my steps nor in Miss O'Flaherty's steps, but to make original footprints of your own. Not everyone is capable of doing so. It requires both heart and brains, though most people think all that is needed is a rent-extracting machine. Indeed, so strained and warped from the true uses have the relations between landlord and tenant become, that even at the best a landlord's in hardly a desirable position. For my own part I have gradually withdrawn from it till I find myself now as little of a landlord as possible on the acres my forefathers owned, and for this I may thank my forefathers themselves, who, as some irreverent wag said the other day, sold my birthright for a mess of *poteen*,[2] and figuratively speaking, gave their souls for a fox

---

2. 'A mess of pottage' was phrase used for a worthless exchange. Here pottage has been replaced by the word for an illegally distilled beverage of high alcoholic content.

hunt.[3] Not that I am an enemy of the hunt; on the contrary; but there are more ways than one of breaking a man's neck by means of the sport. I will show you to-morrow, Miss O'Kelly, if you and Father Daly will give me a seat on his car when you are going your rounds, the house in which your humble servant was born, once a jovial house, an open house, a reckless, rack-renting house as any in old Ireland. The roof is now falling in and the chimneys extend their cold arms to heaven as if crying out against the ruin that has descended upon it. Only that I had a mother—well, you will know my mother by-and by—who preferred a straight conscience and simple living to ancestral halls and all that kind of thing, I should this moment be patching at that family roof-tree, and sending the smoke of unholy feasts up those gaping chimneys. As it is, we have slackened rein on the necks of our tenantry, and in many instances given them the bit in their own teeth. We have here in this island sanctuary, set up our few remaining household gods; and as in our case it was not too late to mend, we have enjoyed infinite peace since we ceased to hold up our heads among the great ones of the earth. Our plan has worked well, I think, though I do not pretend that in trying to do what is best for my people, I have succeeded in satisfying them all. In every community there is more or less of a sinister element which blows like a contrary wind against the prow of all well-meaning efforts. However, I have been content to struggle on in the teeth of such difficulty, remembering how the demon was first evoked in this country and knowing how hard it is to lay a demon, once he has been evoked. Remembering, too, how early in life I myself was misled with too much ardour and cherished a delusion, and had almost descended—"

"We will not speak of that," said Mrs. Kilmartin, with a swift motion of her hand.

"No, we will not speak of that," said Bryan. "I already owe

---

3. Fox hunting on horseback was one of the principal pastimes for the gentry in the Irish countryside.

Miss O'Kelly an apology for my egoism. My only excuse is that I have been led into it through my anxiety for her in her present position. She is placed as I was, somewhat, and is called on to act. I hope she will neither have to run the risks I have run, nor miss her opportunity of doing whatever good she may. I feel that she ought to have the benefit of every one's experience."

"I have already had several varieties," said Marcella. "First, poor Mrs. O'Kelly instructed me carefully from her point of view, next Miss O'Flaherty gave me a great deal of information, as did also Mr. O'Flaherty during the day I spent at Mount Ramshackle. From Mrs. Kilmartin I have heard a great deal that has placed my difficulties plainly before me; and now Mr. Kilmartin—"

Bryan wondered why she smiled at him so incessantly while she spoke, and in the fascination of her smile he now almost forgot the subject of her speech. He did not know that it was to guard his secret, or rather her own secret knowledge of his secret that she smiled, dazzling his eyes with bright glances so that he might not see behind such glamour the melancholy Marcella of the Liberties.

"She must be happy here," he thought. "She must be feeling happy with us. Would to God she could always stay!" and then almost shocked at the vehemence of this wish which was a revelation to himself, he answered quickly:

"I hope you will use all these experiences only as so many lamps to guide your way. I have no doubt your own womanly instinct will find you a path for yourself which nobody has trod before you."

But after they had separated for the night, and all the lights were out in the house, he walked down on the rocks where there was always a murmur of music at night, a faint sweet clashing of sounds in the air, even when storms were still, a mingling of splashing water, whispering reeds, and the cries echoed from shore to shore of wild birds, among the rocks, or riding late on the circling waves that girdle Inisheen. And as he went he thought:

"An impoverished man, one perhaps fatally marked by misfortune, to think of taking possession of the future of a creature so full of life, and freshness, and promise? No, I must not dare to dream of her."

Marcella, meanwhile, followed him with her thought, and asked herself what was that evil from which he had with difficulty been saved, of which his mother would not suffer him to speak? And holding fast the ring round her neck, she fell into a troubled sleep.

CHAPTER TWELVE
DISTRESNA[4]

He who has never ridden on an Irish jaunting-car, a tidy little car with good springs and cushions, drawn by a fast trotting horse, has not travelled so along Irish hilly roads or through Irish green boreens—has missed one of the pleasantest sensations in life. No other vehicle mounts the rugged hill so boldly and easily, and rattles down again so joyously into the hollow of the capricious highway or by-way. No other vehicle affords such easy opportunity for friendly chat between two travellers who sit well back on either seat of the car, leaning towards one another with each an elbow on the "well" cushion. But it is almost as difficult to those not to the manner born to sit a jaunting car as to sit a horse. A certain almost unconscious grasp with the knee and poise of one foot is necessary to give the rider that birdlike sensation of skimming through the air at will which is so utterly unknown to people who drive in carriages.

Father Daly, Bryan, and Marcella, all being to the manner born, pursued their way through the hills as lightly as the breeze blew, till, at a turn of a road, a poor woman suddenly appeared and courtesying in the middle of the path, requested Father Daly to come with her on a sick call.

---

4. 'Distress' was a word used to indicate poverty. The name of the area thus indicates that it is a poor area.

"Well, and who is ill now?"

"Och, yer reverence, it's the ould man himsel."

"Are you sure he hasn't got the toothache like the last time I went and found him bravely?"

"Oh, sorra fear, yer riverence, but he's bad this time. It's convulted altogether he is, an' not expected since six this mornin'."

"Over-eat himself, I suppose," said Father Daly in a tone that gave a pathetic meaning to the seemingly heartless words.

"That's about it, Father Daly," said the woman, understanding.

"I believe he's ready for the road, so. Poor Barney was always a good warrant to love God Almighty," said the priest, solemnly, using the idiom of the people the better to make himself understood.

"Thrue for you, Father Daly, but ye see the terrible state of the politics has druv his prayers a bit out of his mind, an' he's off his religion this while back. An' though I don't mane rightly to say be doesn't love God, still he doesn't pay high encomiums to him the way he used to do, yer riverence, an' he doesn't insinuate afther Him."

"Well, well, I'll go and talk to him a bit, and we'll make that all right again," said Father Daly.

"I'm going off here to a place up the mountain where the people live chiefly on air, and sometimes it disagrees with them," he added, to Marcella. "Sometimes it disagrees with them," he repeated, muttering to himself, as he slid gently down from the car, being no longer of an age to jump off.

"Do you mean that it is a case of starvation?" asked Marcella, eagerly. She knew enough of the pains of want to be quick at guessing what was meant.

"Something of that, something of that. What I would call the slow hunger if I were a doctor and could invent a new disease; not a new one either, but one that belongs to Ireland, as cholera belongs to the East. There now, that will do," as Marcella took a little basket from the well of the car and handed it promptly to Pat. "And now, Bryan, my boy, take the reins yourself and finish the drive, and you can call for me at the Windy Gap when you're jogging homewards. If I'm there an hour too soon it does not matter. Sure I've my breviary in my pocket, and I couldn't read my office in the middle of finer scenery."

And the priest and Pat having set off up a footpath slanting along the face of the overhanging hill, Kilmartin and Marcella continued their journey together.

In spite of his self-warning of the night before, Bryan felt a keen delight in the chance that had given Marcella to his sole keeping for several hours. As they spun along the level roads or walked slowly up the steep hills, the thoughtful look on his face relaxed, and his eyes shone. They two were alone in the brilliant weather, among the blue mountains, breathing the freshest, most exhilarating breezes of heaven, and he found the solitary companionship surpassingly sweet. Nothing draws two spirits, if they are already sympathetic, more closely together than to be placed side by side in some impressive solitude of nature, where under her spell all that is noblest and best in one heart rushes to meet what corresponds with it in the other. Dropping his well-grounded presentiments of coming misfortune behind him like a mantle that impeded his course, Kilmartin went forward through the sunshine, with something of the feelings one would give to a soul newly and unexpectedly arrived in Paradise. As wild, subtle, and penetrating as the odour of the mountain heather on the wind that filled his nostrils was this new influence which overmastered his melancholy humour with its potent delight. Yet so strong was his habit of reserve and self-control that the only sign of the new joy awakened within him lay in the swift changes in his eyes and on his mouth as he flicked with his whip and looked up the enpurpled bluffs and braes, and away into the infinite glories of sky and highland ahead, thrillingly conscious of the nearness of the fair face half turned to him from the other side of the car, yet only allowing himself an occasional glance at it. At last on the top of a hill he stopped the car, and said:

"Now, Miss O'Kelly, if you will stand up for a few minutes, I will show you the lie of this side of Distresna with regard to the lands near it—my own and Mr. O'Flaherty's. I say my own, for though almost all that we can descry from here has passed from my hands into those of peasant proprietors, it is the most precious of all my possessions—I look on it as the very apple of my eye. I am watching with I cannot tell what eagerness to see how the scheme will work."

"Up to the present how has it worked?" asked Marcella, who stood on the footboard of the car, holding the rail with one hand, and with the other shading her eyes from the strong sunlight as she gazed down into the variegated valley in the direction indicated by Bryan with his whip.

"Look through this," he said, giving her a field-glass, "and your own eyes will suggest the answer. To this side, where you see white walls and new thatches, and here and there the absence of offensive heaps by the door, and the beginning of general neatness about, there are some of my small peasant proprietors. Over yonder where you see smoke coming out of the hillside through an old broken basket—that is Distresna, and you will find many of your tenants burrowing thus in the earth, like moles."

"Why?"

"Because, they will tell you, (that is, if they have courage to speak) that the traditions of the country and all the experiences of those who within their own memory have made the trial, go to prove that anyone who makes a show of decency and neatness in his dwelling has his rent raised without fail, before he has had time to reap any benefit himself from his own improvements, and only that he may be forced to clear out and make room for a richer tenant."

"But you had not—you would not have treated them so!"

"I am sorry to say that in my father's time it was done, and they naturally expected me to act like others of my family and class. I found them quite unbelieving and unmanageable on the old lines.

On the new ones—well, already the best of them look on me as their friend."

"And yet, does it not seem a pity to let the old relations of landlord and tenant quite die out?" said Marcella. "It seems to me such a good relation if everyone did his duty."

"With an 'if' what cannot man do? Take the universe to pieces and rebuild it again," said Kilmartin. "Unfortunately men with power too often think more of doing their will than their duty, and in world-forgotten place like this every owner of a few hundred acres has been accustomed to look upon himself as a sultan. As for myself I thought the matter out and put it thus: many men have probably had as generous thoughts in the beginning of their career as those that come to me. How do I know that later in life I shall not have become so attached to some form of selfishness or other that will show me things in a different light from that in which I see them now? I will put it out of my own power to be a persecutor of my fellowmen, even with the most plausible reasoning on my side. I confess that a hereditary liking for the position of landlord has stood in my way, and, even now, if I can possibly save the mastership of the remnant of my property, I feel that I will do it. But not unless I can by this means effect as much improvement as by the other. I will have no slaves living under my rule."

Marcella did not reply. In her heart she leaned to the side of landlordism. It seemed to her that it ought to be so easy for the rich and powerful to take care of the ignorant and poor. She, herself, in her consciousness of a state of general ignorance which she innocently thought must be very peculiar for one in her position as a lady, felt ever inclined to turn to those above her in education and rearing for example and guidance. She was aware too that her exceptional experience of the tribulations of the poor ought to give her (when educated, as she now hoped to be), a particular advantage in the efforts she might make to raise the conditions of those over whom she had been so strangely and wonder fully placed. She felt a strong desire to try her own powers of working good before throwing the reins out of her hands that had as yet hardly grasped them.

"You do not advise me to follow your example, to turn my tenants at once into peasant proprietors?"

"'I advise you to do nothing till you shall see further for yourself. For one thing many of your people are incapable of becoming proprietors until the present state of the law of purchase is amended. You would have to lend money, a certain proportion of the money (to buy your own land), to your purchasing tenant, and afterwards take a mortgage on your own land (yours no longer) as your only security for repayment. In almost all cases this is what I have done, and at the present moment I find it anything but an enriching procedure. In reserving a part of my property, stopping my sales, I act under necessity, as I have no more money to venture, and so feel no scruple at persisting in the role of landlord, to a certain extent. For the rest we shall see. Now, Miss O'Kelly, at which of these underground edifices do you wish to pay a visit?"

By this time they were wending up a by-road, so rutty and uneven that they had had to alight, and walk, one on either side of the horse's head, while the car jolted over stones and into hollows.

"I want to see a Mrs. Conneely who lives about here. I talked to her on the road the other day and promised to come to see her. Ah, there is the young man who was with her. This must be the place."

A shock head was protruded from the hole under the hill, and a voice said:

"Sure it's the young lady hersel' that's come to us. Me sowl! but I knowed she wasn't wan o' the forgettin' sort!"

"At the same time the wail of an infant in pain was heard from the underground cabin.

"Is the baby not better?" asked Marcella of the owner of the shock head, who, having withdrawn it for a few moments, put it forth again.

"Musha it's in heaven any betterment'll be that is for it," said the lad, pulling his wild forelock as he stepped out of the hole and invited the lady in. "Only don't for yer life tell that to the mother o't, Miss."

Marcella could at first see nothing in the cabin, for the smoke which the basket in the chimney-hole failed to carry successfully aloft, but presently she descried a woman on her knees before a kind of cradle made of a *cleeve* (turfcreel),[5] set upon two long dry sods of turf, and heard the reiterated word, half a caress, and half a moan of agony:

"*Acushla machree! Acushla machree! Acushla machree! machree!*"[6]

Marcella waited for a few moments and then put her hand on the woman's shoulder. There is as much difference of expression between one light touch and another, as between gentle tones of voice. The meaning conveyed by the tips of five fingers may be cruel or tender, callous and cold, or exquisitely sympathetic. Marcella's touch found, without jarring, the chord most susceptible of sympathy in the mother's suffering heart.

"What is the matter with him? What can we do for him?" she whispered, kneeling beside the poor woman, and stealing an arm round her.

"Och, it's only the hunger, Miss—he can't ate the yellow male, an' I've nothing else for him. We haven't had a tint o' milk these three days."[7]

The next minute Marcella was warning some milk that she had brought in the car, and was presenting it to the mother, who, after making an effort to speak, had fallen forward again on the cradle, embracing the little white set form it held with both her lean brown arms.

"I think it is only exhaustion, and this may not be too late,"

---

5. A basket for holding and transporting turf.
6. 'My darling heart.'
7. Yellow meal was imported American maize that was sometimes used in Ireland during times of food shortage.

she said. "Let me try," and gently putting the dazed creature aside, Marcella lifted the child in her arms, and, sitting down on a broken stool, began to moisten the infant's lips with the natural nourishment. The pale lips moved and received the fluid, and after a time the eyes opened and seemed to look for more. In a quarter of an hour the child was unmistakably better. Marcella remained yet another half hour nursing, feeding, caressing it, while the mother knelt speechless watching her, no more daring to interfere than if it was the Holy Mother herself who had come down out of heaven and taken her child's case out of her hands. The tall lad with the shock head stood by, his great hollow eyes fixed on Marcella, a look of eager appreciation of the scene on his pallid face. Finally, when the child seemed to fall into a natural sleep, Marcella restored him to his mother's arms.

The poor woman pressed the babe convulsively to her breast, as she took the seat from which her visitor rose, and, not attempting to speak her thanks, merely lifted the hem of Marcella's dress and put it to her lips.

"I will leave you this bottle of milk, and to-morrow I shall send more. Mike will come for it, perhaps," said Marcella, looking in the youth's face as if making a personal request.

Mike's ready, "I will, Miss," nearly choked him. He brushed his hand across his eyes, and escorted the lady from the cabin, and then glanced at her with a kind of reverential rapture as she stood on the grass, looking up and down for Kilmartin, who, having witnessed something of the foregoing scene in the cabin, was now making a meditation upon it at a distance, as he fed Father Daly's little fast trotting horse.

The pig, who had been another witness of the scene within the cabin, now also came forth to see the lady off.

"Why do you not sell *that* rather than be hungry?" asked Marcella of Mike, as the animal stood grunting at her, whether in reproach or thanksgiving, who can tell?

"Is it the pig, Miss? Sure that's the rint. He's all we have betune oursel's an' the cowld mountain side. Whin he goes sure we'll all have to folly him, barrin' he goes into the lan'lord's pocket."

Marcella smiled broadly at the notion of Mike and the pig in her pocket.

"I am going to buy him from you," she said, "and you can keep him for me till the landlord wants him. I will give you the price of him to-morrow when you come. Best market price. Honour bright. And by the way, who is your landlord?"

Mike was so struck dumb not only at this announcement of her intended purchase, but by her peculiar idea of her rights as a purchaser, that he made no answer, only turned crimson up to the roots of his hair.

"Who is the landlord, Mike?" But Mike could not even hear the question, so wildly was the pig still running through his head.

"It's too much, Miss," he blurted out at last. "Sure you don't know how much that baste is worth. The half year's rent's inside of him."

"Seven pounds, Mike."

"Oh musha, Miss, not so much as that." And then, utterly abashed by such magnificent generosity, he hung his head, while his thoughts whirled riotously in the expectation of coming affluence to the family.

"But you have not told me yet, Mike, who is the landlord."

"Sure she's dead, Miss, an' the agent's turned off, and sorra wan owns us this minute, for the new landlord's a lady too, an' we haven't seen her or heard tell of her, an' maybe niver will. But the new agent'll be down on us for the next gale of rint.[8] An' av coorse he'll be harder than the last one."

"Why should he be harder? And how do you know there will be an agent?"

"Ladies always has agents," said Mike, "and the next agent is always worse than the one before. That's all we know about it yet, Miss."

---

8. A gale day was a day on which rent was due.

"Well, Mike, we'll march our pig to meet him when he comes, and we needn't be afraid of him for awhile, anyway," said Marcella, laughing. "But how have you managed up to this?"

"Ye see, Miss, me brother-in-law, that's her husband" (jerking his thumb towards the cabin), "is away in England workin' at the harvest, an' he'll bring a bit o' money home wit him. Meself would ha' been wit him only for the faver I've just riz out of, Miss. I'm the last of a long family meself, an' only for bein' sickly I'd be in America like the rest o' them that sends a pound now and again to help to stop the gap. Sure only that the weather does go dead again us we'd always have potatoes and turf, and could go abroad to airn the rint. But whin the rain rots the potatoes, and there's no dryin' for the turf, an' the yalla male's that dear—och we'd need to be angels wit wings, and no atin' at all, to get on wit it."

"Now what do you think, Mike? Would you not be better off if you were away entirely, all of you to a country where it's easier to get something to eat?"

"Faix,[9] Miss, an' maybe we would. Only I'm thinkin' the ould hills would be lonesome witout some of us. An' there's a power o' us gone already ye see, Miss. There's a power o' us gone already."

Mike did not know what a weighty truth he had uttered. Surely enough the accumulated masses of exiled Irish are proving themselves a terrible power.[10]

The desire to hear the praises of Kilmartin here constrained Marcella to ask a reason for the superior appearance of some of the houses down yonder in the valley.

"Sure that's Mr. Bryan's land, Miss, an' isn't he makin' their own owners of the whole o' them! It's what they call *pisant propriety*,[11] Miss; maybe ye have heard of it?"

---

9. 'Faith!' is a pious exclamation.
10. Irish emigrants were often depicted as exiles, thus rendering their departure as an unjust imposition.
11. 'Peasant proprietorship,' was the eventual outcome to the land war, though this was by no means clear by the mid-1880s.

"He has been good to the people. Do they like him for it?"

Mike lowered his voice. "Sure Miss, they love the ground he walks—barrin' them"—he broke off and looked around him cautiously. "Them that we needn't be mintionin'. There's some that has an ould crow to pluck wit him, an' I'm feared they're on for pluckin' it."

The change in Mike's face was even more remarkable as he spoke his last words than were the words themselves, and as Marcella noted this, her own eyes took such a scared expression, that Mike said suddenly, as if a light had dawned on him:

"Maybe he is somethin' to ye, Miss. I mane, *maybe he has you bespoke*."[12]

Though the words were audacious, the anxious delicacy of Mike's manner of saying them forbade all offence. Marcella coloured, but said frankly.

"Mr. Kilmartin is a friend of mine, but that is all. Nobody has me 'bespoke'."

Mike's countenance brightened. What was it to him, poor lad, what gentleman might have a claim upon the beautiful lady who was as far removed above himself as the stars are above the little bog pools that occasionally reflect them? Yet somehow it pleased poor gaunt, shock-headed, ragged Mike, that this creature of his sudden worship belonged as yet to no man, had, as he might imagine if he liked, no fixed place among the "ginthry," and could wander at her own sweet will among the mountains, as likely to have come down out of the clouds as to have come up out of the lowlands.

Nevertheless, with the quickness of perception of his race and class, he had read in Marcella's eyes that Kilmartin's safety was dear to her; and he said, as Bryan himself was seen leading the horse and car to meet them:

"Tell him to take care o' himsel', Miss, for there's thim that's set

---

12. 'Bespoke' meaning engaged to be married.

to hurt him. Ax him to take a trip to see Amerikay."

There was no time to question him as to the meaning of his ominous words. The next minute Marcella was looking back from her seat on the car, at the wild figure of Mike, as he stood gazing with reverential eyes in the direction towards which her face was set, long after he could see it no more.

With a cold shudder she felt that in return for her exertions a thorn had been planted in her heart, and one which it would be hard to eradicate. She felt indignant at Mike for suggesting what could hardly be true. Had not Kilmartin's fault in the eyes of his friends been only too great a sympathy with the disaffected people, and had not it been made clear to her that any danger threatening him (and, thank God, it was blown over), had loomed from a quarter directly opposite to that now so strangely indicated? How could she convey such a message to Kilmartin's ear? And yet she must not dare to sleep without communicating it to him. As they moved on, Bryan noticed her changed and dejected looks, and said:

"You must not take the sufferings of these poor people too much to heart. Happily, you have the power to alleviate it."

In saying this he was thinking of a power distinct from that which mere money had placed in her hands. But Marcella's thoughts did not follow his words, being quite filled with the idea of his danger, and, thinking her tired, he remarked that it was now too late to pay further visits.

"You gave so much time to that baby," he said, "that if we do not now get on quickly Father Daly will be reading his office in the Windy Gap till it grows too dark to see, even with spectacles."

"But we can easily get home before dark," said Marcella, anxiously, and Kilmartin, wondering at the sudden change in her spirits urged the horse to a faster trot. As they spun along the road in silence the girl's mind was distracted with doubts and questions. Ought she not to put him on his guard at once, and yet why should she spoil the drive which he was so evidently enjoying, and bring back the cloud of care to his eyes which were shining on her now with a happy tenderness? She hated to be the messenger of evil to him; and, after all, did she not utterly disbelieve in the vague warning which she had got to give him? Of course it must be given. She would not take the risk of withholding it. But there was no need to think of it now, not till these beautiful moments of travel and companionship should be displaced by the inevitable future, and pushed back to the greedy past gaping for them.

Kilmartin, having felt the mountain-air grow keener as they ascended the pass leading to the road by which they were to return towards Inisheen, wrapped her in a woollen shawl, and then set himself to beguile her fatigue with stories of the country through which they were passing.

"Over yonder, Miss O'Kelly, is the old home of the Kilmartins, the house in which I was born. Does not it present a wild spectacle, a striking instance of the thrift of Irish landlords, for you see when that roof-tree began to decay rents were paid, and those who received them ought to have been able to keep the wolf from the door. In that old house what dreams I have dreamed. As a lad, I felt that there was something terribly wrong in the existing state of things, and I wanted to redeem Ireland. My mother, as you have discovered, has warm national blood in her veins. Some of her family fled to France long ago and joined the Irish brigades there.[13] Almost all of her people are exiles through political causes in the past, and she, God bless her, fed me on Irish history and poetry, while my father, good easy man, thought of little besides his hunt and his hunt-dinner, and his flowing punch-bowl. The consequence was that I even went beyond my mother in ardour for the Irish cause, and at seventeen, rushed into the arms of the Fenians."

---

13. After the treaty of Limerick (1691) and into the eighteenth century many Irish soldiers left for the continent where they entered the service of European powers, often in special Irish units.

Marcella, uttered a little cry of dismay.

Kilmartin smiled. "You needn't be frightened," he said, "I am not a Fenian now. My mother discovered the matter and appealed to my father, and I was sent to Cambridge, and afterwards to travel. In the course of a few years I had learned to think; and, though my enthusiasm for Ireland was no way cooled, I saw the folly and wickedness of dreams of war which had not the remotest chance of success. Since then I have turned my attention to the consideration of more rational ways of benefiting my country than those proposed by Fenianism, which, though it began with a bold scheme for war, has, I am sorry to say, degenerated so far as to identify itself with societies for assassination. I shook myself free of it with some trouble and at some risk, but over yonder, Miss O'Kelly, in that romantic little green hollow between two purple hills, is the spot where we used to drill. Convert as I am to sane and peaceful aims, grown old in wisdom and experience, I can yet feel the thrill of an exquisite sense of daring and danger, the strong rapture in the vivid hope of one day marching to battle for Faith and Fatherland to win a triumph which was to be followed by the blossoming of the wilderness and food in plenty for the famishing. All the heroic patriots of antiquity were my models, and I may well regret the passing of the youthful fervour of spirit that brought me yonder in the silence of a moonlight night, my gun on my shoulder, my heart beating like a martial drum, and my mind fixed on the determination to risk individual destruction for the sake of the future of my race."

Marcella was silent. From all this revelation she had gained a few ideas. In the first place, he had really been a Fenian, and in the second place, by renouncing Fenianism, he had incurred the enmity of that formidable body. From which side now did his danger proceed, a danger of which he himself was perhaps this moment in ignorance? Was it as a former Fenian, an offender against the law, or as a seceder from the secret society that he had become a mark for vengeance at unknown hands? His escape from the police on that memorable night seemed to point to the one, and the warning given by Mike implied the other. If a mingling of the two might be imagined—

Here a sharp turn of the road brought them into the Windy Gap, and Father Daly climbed upon the car. Then Marcella made an effort to rally her spirit, and related the experiences of the drive to his reverence.

Father Daly rubbed his hands in delight. "Capital!" be cried, "capital! What will become of the poor creatures with joy when they find whom they have got for their landlord?"

"The priest returned with them to Inisheen for the night, and after dinner, at his urgent cry for a little music, Mrs. Kilmartin's harp was carried to the side of her couch, and she sang for the little company.

"Only Bryan and Father Daly would listen to an old woman's song," she said to Marcella; "they have so long been accustomed to hear me that they will not allow either the voice or the harp-strings to be cracked. As for you, my dear, you will have to try to be patient."

"Give us the *Wild Geese*," said Father Daly.[14] "Miss O'Kelly, the song which Mrs. Kilmartin sings for me every time I come here, was translated from the Irish, long ago, by an ancestress of hers, whose lover had to fly the country, and whom she never saw again."

The little white-haired lady sitting up on her sofa touched her instrument as if with fairy fingers and a wild flowing melody that sounded to Marcella's ears like fitful weeping trickled over the harp strings.

---

14. The Wild Geese were aristocratic Catholic Irish émigrés to Europe, many of them soldiers, in the wake of the Jacobite defeat and the Treaty of Limerick (1691). The lyrics to the song appear to be a poem of Mulholland's own composition and appears in her collection, *Vagrant Verses* (London: Elkin Mathews, [1899]), pp. 18–20.

I had no sail to cross the sea,
A brave white bird went forth from me,
My heart was hid beneath his wing:
O strong white bird, come back in spring!

I watched the wild geese rise and cry
Across the flaring western sky,
Their winnowing pinions clove the light,
Then vanished, and came down the night.

I laid me low, my day was done,
I longed not for the morrow's sun,
But closely swathed in swoon of sleep,
Forgot to hope, forgot to weep.

The moon through veils of gloomy red,
A warm yet dusky radiance shed,
All down our valley's golden stream,
And flushed my slumber with a dream.

Her mystic torch lit up my brain,
My spirit rose and lived amain,
And followed through the windy spray
That bird upon its watery way.

O wild white bird, O wait for me,
My soul hath wings to fly with thee,
On foam waves lengthening out afar,
We'll ride toward the western star.

O'er glimmering plains through forest gloom,
To track a wanderer's feet I come,
'Mid lonely swamp, by haunted brake,
I'll pass unfrighted for his sake.

Alone, afar, his footsteps roam,
The stars his roof, the tent his home,
Saw'st thou what way the wild geese flew
To sunward through the thick night dew?

Carry my soul where he abides,
And pierce the mystery that hides
His presence, and through time and space
Look with mine eyes upon his face.

Beside his prairie fire he rests,
All feathered things are in their nests:
"What strange wild bird is this, he saith,
Still fragrant with the ocean's breath?

"Perch on my hand, thou briny thing,
And let me stroke thy shy wet wing;
What message in thy soft eye thrills?
I see again my native hills,

"And vale, the river's silver streak,
The mist upon the blue, blue peak,
The shadows grey, the golden sheaves,
The mossy walls, the russet eaves.

"I greet the friends I've loved and lost,
Do all forget? No, tempest-tost,
That braved for me the ocean's foam,
Some heart remembers me me at home.

"Ere spring's return I will be there,
Thou strange sea fragrant messenger!"
I wake and weep; the moon shines sweet,
O dream too short! O bird too fleet!

"It is too long for a song," said Mrs. Kilmartin, having finished. "No one but Father Daly would willingly listen to more than three stanzas. The length of 'Silent, O Moyle,' is the length for a perfect song." And she sang Moore's exquisite melody.[15]

"Delicious!" murmured Father Daly, with a long sigh of enjoyment. "Now, Bryan, where is your fiddle?"

An instrument was produced and handed first to the old man, who played an Irish planxty of Carolan's, mad with fun and frolic.[16] Afterwards the fiddle was passed to Bryan, in whose hands it became the violin—

> "That small sweet thing,
> Devised in love and fashioned cunningly
> Of wood and strings."[17]

Bryan touched it with the skill of an artist and, in a little theme of Beethoven, made it give forth the soul of the musician.[18] Marcella, whose nerves were already over strung, was almost wrought to tears by the divine tenderness of his music. Over and above Beethoven the cry of the Wild Geese was in her heart. "Tell him to go a trip to see Amerikay," said Mike. Was he too destined to be a wanderer far from the land he loved so well, or be sacrificed to some cruel alternative? She could not dare to sleep without delivering her warning, and wrote a few words in pencil on a page in her pocketbook, while Mrs. Kilmartin and the priest were talking, and Bryan was still playing.

As they separated for the night she put it into his hand unobserved, and greatly astonished he held it folded in his palm until he found himself alone.

---

15. "Silent, O Moyle" was published in volume two of the *Irish Melodies* (1820–1) by Thomas Moore (1779–1852).
16. Turlough O'Carolan (1670–1738) was a blind Irish harper. A planxty is an Irish dance tune played on the harp.
17. Concluding lines from 'Music' by George Laurin, though in the original the first word is 'this'.
18. German composer Ludwig van Beethoven (1770–1827).

Having read the few urgent words in Marcella's large rather unformed handwriting, he looked at first more glad than alarmed, then asked himself was it fancy or conceit that led him to discern an accent of piteous fear for his safety in the imaginary voice in which the written message was delivered. Would she greatly care if he were hurt? If so, it were almost good to be hurt.

He remembered her sudden fit of dejection after quitting Mike, and the suggestion that anxiety for him had caused it, came to him with so much sweetness that it was some time before he could cease to dwell on it and give his attention to the warning itself.

Then, "I am not surprised," he reflected, "but I stand my ground. The danger does not blow from the quarter Mike apprehends. It may be that it were better if it did. But at all events I stand my ground."

Then studying again the simple words on the scrap of paper in his hand, he forgot the cause of his getting them in the joy of their possession.

CHAPTER THIRTEEN
MARCELLA, A LANDLORD

For some time after this Marcella's hands were full of business. What with taking measures to make Crane's Castle habitable, and continuing her visits to her tenantry in company with Father Daly, or Kilmartin, or both, she had little idle time. With a few bold assured words Bryan had almost set her mind at rest on the subject of danger to him, so that she was able to give at least a good part of her thoughts to putting her affairs in order, and laying a foundation for a future happy understanding between her people and herself.

Gradually the poor dwellers on the green spots between the bogs and the barren stretches of mountain came to look for the visits of the smiling lady who was "that kind, you wouldn't think she was a lady at all," and the pinched weather-beaten faces would brighten at her approach, and the little brown bare-legged children in their scanty garments of crimson home-spun flannel would come capering like wild goats along the rocks to meet her. By degrees all the cases of hardship, the evictions, and rent-raisings were laid before her.[19] Sitting at the cabin fires while the old granny in the corner smoked the tobacco the lady had brought, and Marcella, herself, helped to drink the tea which had been transferred from her own pocket to the little brown teapot on the hearth, she became acquainted with all the ills to which these suffering creatures had been subjected, that her rent-roll might show an increase rather than a falling off in wealth. Since Mrs. O'Kelly, five years ago, had shaken the dust of Distresna off her feet (offended at some complaints that had been made of what she sincerely considered her most benignant rule), and departed from Crane's Castle never to return, the agent had been gradually screwing up the rents, trying to extract a little more and a little more money out of bog and rock; and at the same time the seasons had been wet and cruel, turf had not been dried and potatoes had failed, and a good part of the hard-earned rent, earned in America, England, anywhere, had been spent on the insufficient yellow-meal on which the defaulters all but starved. There had been several evictions within the year before Mrs. O'Kelly's death. In some cases the ruined families had disappeared from the country, in others they lived among their neighbours, while a son or daughter had gone as a sort of advanced guard to America to try to earn some money which might get them reinstated in their holdings. A few dwellings better than ordinary, showing signs of improvement at the cost of much labour, were pointed to as warnings to the wise man not to improve. Out of these the rash and adventurous improvers had been cast to repent of their folly, the young in exile, the old in the poorhouse.[20]

As Marcella listened and observed, her heart was stirred,

---

19. Evictions, or removing tenants from their farms for nonpayment of rent was a particular source of grievance.
20. An informal name for a workhouse, a residential state facility for the poor.

and she remembered that she also was a child of the people. If through her mother she was descended from the gentry who had so mismanaged and misruled these poor, through her father she was one with them. The power to alleviate their wants and their miseries had been wonderfully placed in her hands; the will should not be wanting. With unfailing patience she studied their various cases, learned their views, perceived and appreciated their temptations.

With the landlord on the one side, irritating and crushing them, and on the other, the secret societies pressing them to put themselves in the hands of a power that declared itself able and willing to right them, was it surprising if the more desperate among them fell blindly into complicity with crime? The only wonder was that the bulk of them kept free from it. Can one be astonished that the Fenian's promise of a warfare that should bring glorious changes over the face of the country, should have enthralled the more sturdy and fearless of the youth, taught them to shoulder a gun, and enticed them to the secret meeting-place in the heart of the moonlit glen? On these things Marcella mused and pondered. If Bryan, as a lad, had been inspired to rush out from his mother's side in his comfortable home, to strive to right the wronged, how much more those whose aged parents or little children were wasting before their eyes in the very grip of the wrong?

Well, she would have no more Fenians, no more slaves, no more starvation, no more eviction. Her rent-roll should be to her but as a calendar of good deeds done. In one spot of Ireland at least, prosperity as great as the poverty of the land would permit, should reign. To Crane's Castle should come all who needed help or comfort. With their babies in her arms, their children about her knees, she would know how to talk to the mothers and fathers.

In the meantime the people were full of anxiety about their new landlord, and Marcella was often questioned as to whether she had heard anything about that person, or, more important still, anything of the appointment of an agent. They had learned that Crane's Castle was getting cleaned up and put to rights, and this looked as though the agent, if not the lady herself, intended to live on the property.

In all probability, they thought, the rents would be raised, as a first step, by the new management. How many of those who now clung with passion to their hearths and homes, poor and humble as they might be, would, in a few weeks hence have received the order to go forth, an order which to many was a veritable death sentence. Marcella could tell them nothing, only begged them to hope. To ask them to be patient was unnecessary. Nowhere in the world is such Christian patience to be met with as in an Irish cabin.

In the meantime Crane's Castle was getting thoroughly swept and garnished. The cobwebs of years were blown away, the mouldy old furniture was polished up, pretty new things arrived from Dublin to make the place more comfortable and habitable than it had ever been before, and at last it was ready for Marcella to take possession. A lady of good family, one of the many Irish ladies whose slender income, being derived from a mortgage on land, has vanished of late years, had accepted the position of companion to the heiress of Distresna, and was ready at any moment to obey a summons to the spot. All things were in proper trim when Marcella unfolded her little plan for the conclusion of the play she had been enacting for the benefit of her people.

On a bright Sunday morning in July, it was announced by Father Daly, from the altar in his chapel at Ballydownvalley, that the new landlord, who, as they knew, was a lady, a relative of the late Mrs. O'Kelly, would meet her tenants at Crane's Castle on a certain day in the following week, and would receive their rents in person and hear their complaints, if they had any to make. Now the people upon whom this news fell like a shock, had never known Marcella by any other name than Miss Marcella, and had not the faintest suspicion that she was a personage of importance. A moaning murmur from the women at their prayers greeted the announcement, groups stood late in the chapel yard that day discussing the expected event, and old and young returned to their cabins in the afternoon with a load on their hearts. They had not a doubt among them that the new state of things would be worse than the old, and even Father Daly's silence as to the lady's character and intentions had an ominous meaning for them. If he had been able to say a good word for the new landlord he would surely have done so. All his sermon was about patience and confidence in God, just such a sermon as he had always preached to them when the turf would not dry, and the potatoes failed, or when anybody died of the slow hunger, or was evicted.

On the appointed day they were all in motion on the road to Crane's Castle, that is all the heads of families, or the member of a family who was to act as spokesman for the rest. Crane's Castle stood about a mile from the lake of Inisheen with its face to seaward and a mountain at its back, a quaint ancient building with thick grey walls and small deep-set windows, and a general look about it as if the crows had been building in its chimneys ever since they came out of the Ark. Indoors a mighty change was already noticeable, a few richly coloured rugs on the tiles of the great square vault-like hall and a fire burning on the hearth to consume the damps within and without, gave promise of a cheerful interior. Faded and mildewed carpets and curtains had gone out with the dust accumulated upon them, and the once mouldy and gloomy reception rooms had been so draped, and painted, and garnished, as to have become places to linger in for comfort and repose. In the drawingroom sat Marcella's chaperone, a majestic and handsome woman who plied her embroidery needle with the air of a fallen empress, and never failed to remind all comers that she was "one of the O'Donovans." The last of a dynasty whose subjects had revolted and dethroned her could not have alluded to her misfortunes with more dignified bitterness than did Miss O'Donovan when speaking of the failure of her annuity which had been drawn from a charge upon land. As her case was indeed a hard one (and there are many of such) she was treated with the utmost tenderness by her friends, and Marcella in nominally accepting her services, was prepared to accord her all that unhesitating homage to which her pride and her poverty laid urgent and constant claim.

Of the library, where until now *The Peerage, Burke's Landed Gentry*,[21] and innumerable bound volumes of the sporting papers had been the chief ornaments of the shelves, Marcella had chosen to make her own particular sanctum, and here she awaited her tenants on that day in July. All the earliest arrived were invited to take seats in the hall while the first man was called by name to the presence of the landlord.

They knew that library door too well, having never entered it without fear in their hearts. The first who went in now was quickly aware of a change in the place. There were, as of old, the two high-set narrow windows at the end of the room, but in their recesses and catching the sunshine, stood deep-coloured jars full of tall yellow flag-lilies, filling the niches with brilliance and light. In the shadow between the russet-tinted curtains, a lady was sitting. Her head was bent down, and the heavy-hearted tenant could not see her face. The room was full of flowers, the furniture was the same and yet changed, the poor man gazed round the place with a vague wonder in his mind as to whether the new landlord was as different from the old as this beautiful apartment was the reverse of its former gloomy self. Then he looked again and saw Marcella smiling at him from the shadows between the golden lilies in the windows.

"You see it is me whom you have got for your landlord, and you must make the best of me. Now state your case that we may get to business," she said; and Father Daly here appeared rubbing his hands and laughing with delight.

"John Lynch," he said, "confess that you are sold. Go and tell your neighbours what a terrible landlord has come to Distresna."

---

21. Reference books concerning the aristocracy and landed gentry.

In a few minutes the room was full of the people pressing round Marcella, begging to touch her hand, pouring out their *cead mile failthes* and blessings on her head.[22] It was long before the excitement had subsided and business was begun. All that day and many days after the new landlord sat in her place between the yellow lilies, making a picture in the shadowy old room, listening to the cases laid before her, distributing justices, promising help, lowering rents and granting new leases. After all the business was done her rent roll was considerably disfigured, but her heart was more at rest. Were not these poor over-joyed creatures her actual children? Had they not been given bodily into her charge? Had not Providence ordained that enough sustenance should be derived from the land for her and for them also? Should she store up all the grain for herself and leave nothing for them but the husks? Forbid it, righteous God!

Her next step was to invite the tenantry, men, women, and children, all who could come, to a house warming at Crane's Castle. The great barn and outhouses were cleared for dancing and decorated with heather. Pipers were hired, and a supper was prepared such as the tenants of Distresna had never seen before. Invitations were sent to the gentry also to be present at the Peoples' Ball; but few of them were at home, and still fewer cared to come. Already many heads were shaken over Miss O'Kelly's stranger beginnings with her tenantry. But what could be expected of her seeing she had identified herself from the first with those queer half-Fenian Kilmartins? Yet the dance went on as merrily as though under the patronage of a queen. Marcella danced with her tenants and helped them with her own hands to the good cheer she had prepared for them. The children undertook to teach her the step of the Irish jig, while Father Daly looked on and applauded, and the crowd stood back to watch the performance with delight.

---

22. Irish for 'a hundred thousand welcomes', a greeting.

When the step was learned she danced it with Mike, the mountain lad who had frightened her with his unnecessary warnings.

"Mike," she said, when the jig was finished, "that was all a mistake—I mean your fear that there was harm in store for Mr. Kilmartin."

"I hope so, Miss—I hope so," said Mike, but his beaming looks of pride and joy at being danced with by "herself" vanished like the sun under a cloud. "All the same, there's people here to-night that I do not like the looks of. There's a party in the hayloft and bad scran[23] to the dance they have danced, nothing but chattin' under their breath and dark looks for anybody else that goes near them. One of them's a stranger in these parts and the others are no credit to them they belong to. But whisht, Miss, whisht! Sure we ben't to take notice o' them. It's Mike will keep watch for himsel' and yoursel', an' if danger comes back on the wind, he'll run before everything else with the news of it."

---

23. Bad scran means bad luck.

4

'Wanted an Irish Novelist.'
Irish Monthly. 1891.

Introduction

This article by Mulholland is introduced by Matthew Russell and concluded by him with a quotation from a letter to an American newspaper praising her work. Russell's purpose is to include and to give a high place to Mulholland in the pantheon of Irish writers, as she does not refer to herself in the article. Mulholland's piece itself gives an assessment and listing of Irish writers and concludes with an extract from chapter thirty-two of *The Collegians* (1829) by Gerald Griffin (1803–40), of which she thinks highly. The scene depicts Mr Daly's grief on learning of the death of his wife. Details of almost all of the other writers mentioned in Mulholland's article can be found in James H. Murphy, *Irish Novelists and the Victorian Age* (2011).

The article is important not only because of its listing of authors but, more particularly, because of its call for Irish authors to write about Irish themes. The listing of the best Irish writers had been something of a vogue at the time. However, Mulholland's call for Irish writers to write about and live in Ireland anticipates W.B. Yeats's articles in the *Bookman* in 1895 in which he argued that because of Ireland's underdeveloped cultural position Irish writing had to be about Ireland if it was to be Irish.[1] Mulholland laments the fact that writers who begin writing about Ireland go to live in London and focus on success in the British market. In one sense her perspective is more realistic than Yeats's as it acknowledges the financial dimension to the issue, though she found herself in an unusually fortunate position in being financially secure living in Ireland and, because of the way her early career had developed, able to write about Irish topics and be published in Britain. Ironically, one of the writers Mulholland takes to task was Richard Dowling (1846–98) who was to die in abject poverty in London some years after her piece was published.[2]

1891 Introduction to 'Wanted an Irish Novelist' by Matthew Russell

The writer of the following paper, which we rescue from an American journal of two years ago, labours under the very great disadvantage of being compelled to ignore the existence of an Irish novelist to whom any other but herself would have given the most prominent place among the Irish novelists of our day. In fact, Mr. W. B. Yeats, compiling for G. B. Putnam's Sons of New York and London, two volumes of "Irish Tales" for their exquisite Knickerbocker Nuggets, gives not a single line from any living writer except Miss Rosa Mulholland; and of hers he gives in full that most pathetic little tale, "A Hungry Death," introducing it with this remark: "Miss Mulholland is the novelist of contemporary Catholic Ireland. She has not the square-built power of our older writers, Banim, Carleton, and their tribe, but has, instead, much fancy and style of a sort commoner in our day than theirs, and a distinction of feeling and thought peculiar to herself."

---

1. James H. Murphy, 'The Dark Arts of the Critic: Yeats and William Carleton,' in Marjorie Howes and Joseph Valente (eds), *Yeats and Afterwords* (Notre Dame: Notre Dame University Press, 2014), pp. 80–99.
2. Murphy, *Irish Novelists*, pp. 248–9.

Our readers will, therefore, bear in mind the initials appended to this paper as explaining the strange omission of any allusion to "Marcella Grace," or "A Fair Emigrant," or "The Wild Birds of Killeevy," or "The Wicked Words of Tobereevil," or "Hester's History," or "The Late Miss Hollingford," or any of the countless smaller tales and sketches which often condense into a dozen page more of quiet humour, quiet pathos, and vivid picturesqueness, than can be found in many successful volumes. (Matthew Russell, S.J.)

'Wanted An Irish Novelist'

Another year has come and gone without bringing us the novelist we are hoping for, whom we are in need of, to show us ourselves as we are, neither flattered nor yet too much over shadowed by lack of discernment and sympathy. Every nation has its novelists, and the art has not yet reached its highest development, the art which reflects men and women in their dealings with and attitudes towards each other, revealing their faults and failings, powers and weaknesses, with something added from the artist of suggestion, criticism, idealism, of the reverse which shall help the student to recognise himself or his neighbour, and hit a useful lesson home. The roll-call of Irish novelists is far too short and unsatisfactory, and if it be true that the growth of the novel increases with the prosperity and consequent intellectual culture of a country, we have not far to seek for the reason of our poverty in art.

A few treasures have been handed down to us from the past, works which have made record of the people and ways and scenes of a day gone by. We have the novels of Gerald Griffin, the Banims, Carleton, Miss Edgeworth, Lady Morgan, Lever—all of which give us lively and characteristic pictures of an Ireland we see not now. In later years, either because imagination has grown dull among us, or the ways of life supply less attractive material, or the ready English market for fiction draws off our talent and employs it at remunerative wages on the themes its daily supply requires, for some one or all of these reasons, certain it is that our Irish literature does not become enriched as time goes on, and we shall have little to show for the work of our period at the close of the nineteenth century.

It is a noticeable fact that writers who produce one good Irish novel, giving promise of store to come, almost invariably cease to be Irish at that point, and afterwards cast the tributary stream of their powers into the universal river of English fiction. Thus Mr. Lewis Wingfield, having given us that fine picture of Ireland in the day of the "Volunteers," *My Lords of Strogue*, turned his back upon us, and became in consequence less distinguished and less interesting in his work.[3] Mr. Richard Ashe King in like manner having delighted Irish readers with the *Wearing of the Green*, now supplies an English novel to an English periodical, hiding his shamrock in a field of common clover. Mr. Justin McCarthy also writes perfect English for the English, and the clever books of Mrs. Cashel Hoey show no trace of the fact that she is Irish of the Irish, not only by birth, but in faithful affection. Mr. Richard Dowling, who in his early days of delicate promise migrated to London, and pitched his tent beside the publishers, would doubtless have given us much more beautiful and delicate work if he had stayed within hearing of Shandon Bells.[4] Yet how can we quarrel with any of these bright spirits if they prefer to live their lives pleasantly and in affluent circumstances in the busy, working, paying world of London, rather than content themselves with the ideally uncomfortable conditions of him who elects to chew the cud of sweet and bitter Irish fancies, with his feet in an Irish bog and his head in a rainbow? To choose the latter, very much self-denial is needed, much faith, much singleness of purpose, and

---

3. The Volunteers were an Irish Protestant military group at the end of the eighteenth century.
4. The bells of St Anne's Church, Cork, which feature in a famous song and thus serve as a synecdoche for the city of Cork.

also the sacrifice, sometimes, of things even more sacred than ideal service of country. We must only hope that there will soon come to Ireland the dawn of a new era, when increased prosperity and civilisation will bring increase of artistic culture and a taste for letters, which is at present deplorably wanting in the Irish public. Until such a taste be engendered, we have little chance of possessing a rich literature of our own.

Of the few Irish writers who continue to write for Ireland are Miss Laffan and the clever author of *Hurrish*.[5] While paying large tribute to the brilliant author of *Flitters, Tatters, and the Counsellor* we must regret that her pen is not more often dipped in the milk of human kindness when describing the faults and shortcomings of her worser fellow-countrymen.[6] A little of Thackeray's sly humour and sweetening tenderness would enhance the value of her often just criticism, and a bright picture placed beside a dark one would relieve the somberness of her presentations and more completely reflect the truth. The author of *Hurrish* [Emily Lawless] has also chosen the rôle of censor, though, perhaps, in a less marked degree. All honour to those who dare to expose the naked truth with honest purpose. Would we had a George Eliot to give us of Irish life scenes and characters corresponding to those in *Silas Marner* and *The Mill on the Floss*.[7]

There is no doubt that *The Collegians*, by Gerald Griffin, is the best Irish novel as yet written. Strikingly dramatic, wrought to a fine point of tragedy through varying scenes of the most touching pathos, the most playful humour, every touch is Irish to the life; laughter and tears follow one another as one turns the pages of the book. The entire narrative of the death and funeral of Kyrle Daly's

---

5. Emily Lawless (1845–1913).
6. May Laffan, Lady Harley (1849–1916) was the author of *Flitters, Tatters and the Counsellor* (1879) but also of novels satirical of the Irish Catholic middle classes, such as *Hogan M.P.* (1876).
7. George Eliot was the pen name of the English author Mary Anne Evans (1819–80), author of *Silas Marner* (1861) and *The Mill on the Floss* (1860).

mother thrills with that simple pathos which is of the most perfect art, and no one could read it without the surprise of tears suddenly rushing from the heart. As for instance, the following passage: —

A hurried trampling of feet was now heard in the bedroom, and the sound of rapid voices in anxiety and confusion. A dead silence sank upon the hall. Mr. Daly and his son exchanged a glance of thrilling import. A low moan was the next sound that proceeded from the room. The husband placed the child in the arms of the old woman, and hurried to the chamber door. He was met at the threshold by his sister, Mrs. O'Connell (a grave-looking lady in black), who placed her hands against his breast, and said. with great agitation of manner: "—Charles, you must not come in yet." "Why so, Mary? Low is she?" "Winny!" said Mrs. O'Connell, addressing the old woman who held the infant; "take the child into the kitchen until the nurse can come to you." "How is Sally?" repeated the anxious husband. "You had better go into the parlour, Charles. Recollect yourself now, my dear Charles, remember your children." The old man began to tremble. "Mary," he said, "why will you not answer me? How is she?" "She is not better, Charles." "Not better?" "No, far otherwise." "Far otherwise? Come, woman! let me pass into the room." "You must not, indeed, you must not, Charles!" exclaimed his sister, flinging her arms round his neck and bursting into tears. "Kyrle, Kyrle speak to him!" Young Daly caught his father's arm. "Well, well," said the latter, with a calm, yet ghastly smile, "if you are all against me, I must, of course, submit." "Come with me to the parlour," said Mrs. O'Connell, "and I will explain to you." She took him by the arm, and led him, with a vacant countenance and passive demeanour, through the silent and astonished group. They entered the parlour, and the door was closed by Mrs. O'Connell. Kyrle Daly remained fixed like a statue, in the same attitude in which his aunt had left him, and a moment of intense and deep anxiety ensued. The rare and horrid sound, the scream of an old man in suffering, was the first that broke on that portentous stillness. It acted like a spell on the group in the hall. They were dispersed in an instant. The women ran shrieking in various directions. The men looked dismayed, and uttered hurried sentences of wonder and affright. The children, terrified by the confusion, added their shrill and helpless wailings to the rest. The death-cry re-echoed in the bedroom, in the parlour, and in the kitchen. From every portion of the dwelling the funeral shriek ascended to the heavens, and death and sorrow, like armed conquerors, seemed to have possessed themselves by sudden storm of this little hold, where peace and happiness had reigned so long and so calmly.

The nurse left the kitchen, and Lowry took his seat upon the settle-bed, where he remained for some time looking downwards, and striking the end of his walking stick against the floor, gently and at regular intervals. The crying of the child disturbed his meditations, and he frequently lifted his head and stared with a look of stern remonstrance at the unconscious innocent. "The Lord forgive you, you little disciple," said Lowry; "'tis little you know what harm you have done this day! Do all you can—grow up as fine as a queen, and talk like an angel—'twill set you to fill up the place o' the woman you took away from us this day. Howld your tongue again, I tell you, 'tis we that have raison to cry, an' not you."

The best Irish story written in later years is Miss Keary's *Castle Daly*. Unhappily, the author did not live long enough after its publication to give us another of the same character. — R. M.

Epilogue by Matthew Russell, introducing a letter to the *Boston-Pilot* about Mulholland's piece.

Since sending the preceding pages to the printer we have chanced upon an old *Boston-Pilot*, in which Mr. Francis Nugent, of Peabody, Massachusetts, "supplies the ellipsis" to which we refer in our introductory note. His speaking of *When We Were Boys* as a forthcoming work shows that this letter is already ancient history. If written up to date, there would be some reference to Hannah

Lynch's *Prince of the Glades*, to Oscar Wilde's *Dorian Gray*, and some other Irish work of recent dates. We omit some sentences in which Mr. Nugent ventures to look to Miss Mulholland as "the George Eliot who will give us of Irish life scenes and characters corresponding to those in *Silas Marner* and *The Mill on the Floss*." He begins by telling the Editor of *The Pilot* that he has rarely read cleverer letters than, &c., &c.

That on "Recent Irish Novelists" is extremely interesting, albeit the writer is guilty therein of a few sins of omission. Modesty would not permit her to mention one whose name is a household word wherever the Irish race has found a home. Rosa Mulholland, if not the greatest living Irish novelist, is the best-known Irish writer of the present day. There are very few prose writings of the kind that interest us as do those of Miss Mulholland. There is a certain easy playfulness and gaiety about them, a winning grace, an intuitive insight into nature, and a facility of word-painting which is charming to everybody. "The Wicked Woods of Tobereevil," "Hester's History," "The Wild Birds of Killeevy," and "A Fair Emigrant," are tales of great purity, simplicity and beauty. "Marcella Grace," her best Irish novel, by its captivating naturalness and grace and simplicity, by its representations of real life so vividly true to nature and so home-like, and by its constant yet incidental (so incidental as to seem almost accidental) teachings of the purest and loveliest morality, really charms us. Our mother friend, if we might venture to advise you, we would say that "The Little Flower-Seekers," "The Walking Trees," "Four Little Mischiefs," and "Puck and Blossom," are the stories for your child to read as well as for yourself. Miss Mulholland's "Vagrant Verses" have the same unmistakable impress of originality and power as her prose. Her poetry is all serious, much of it religious. It is of the earnest, dignified, genuine character which commands profound respect, while it stirs a strong enthusiasm. None of it is frivolous—none of it superficial. Some may feel a lack of a gushing spontaneity, a glad, fresh, inspiring liveliness, and may be repelled by a certain stateliness of style. But liveliness is too common to be greatly missed, and dignity, depth, and elaborateness too rare to be lightly prized. Miss Mulholland omits to mention in her list of Irish novelists her sister, Clara Mulholland, author of many pleasant and profitable tales for the young folks; William O'Brien, whose forthcoming novel will create a sensation in literary circles; John Boyle O'Reilly, who has written one of the greatest novels of the present time— "Moondyne," in which the delineations of character are deliciously genial and acute; Mrs. J. H. Riddell, author of a large number of well-conceived and vigorously-written novels, who, in addition to skill in narrative, has powers of describing scenery of no common order; Charlotte Grace O'Brien, daughter of the Irish patriot, William Smith O'Brien, author of "Light and Shade," a well-written novel, which contains passages of exquisite beauty and pathos; and Mrs. Sigerson, whose "Ruined Race" is a vivid but too mournful picture of one phase of Irish life.

5

Nanno, A Daughter of the State.
London, Grant Richards, 1899.

Chapters Fifteen to Seventeen

Introduction

Nanno Breen has had a baby without being married. She leaves the baby behind in the workhouse, or poor house as it is called in the story, where she has long lived, in order to forge a more respectable life for herself in Youghal. She forges a testimonial from Father Tom Shannon who has been kind to her. She is employed by Steve Barron, who has returned from America, on his farm, to the disquiet of Mary Cassidy who hopes to marry him. Steve and Nanno fall in love and become engaged. Chapter Fifteen deals with the repercussions of this decision in the locality. In Chapter Sixteen Nanno struggles with the realization that her position of respectability is based on lies, including the assertion that she is the widow of a sailor and mother of his child. In Chapter Seventeen she goes to retrieve her son from the workhouse in Dublin. She also visits Father Shannon who urges her to tell Steve the truth but she is determined not to and to go ahead with the wedding. In the latter stages of the novel Nanno breaks off with Steve without telling him the real reason but to Father Shannon's approval. Steve marries Mary Cassidy. Nanno receives a marriage proposal from a man who knows the truth about her situation. She refuses to marry him, though she is grateful for his friendship.

As has been noted in the general introduction to this volume, Mulholland took something of a risk with this novel. It challenges the Victorian norm of respectability with the Catholic teaching of a fresh start after repentance and forgiveness. Yet Mulholland ensures that this conflict is never brought to a head, as Nanno's fresh start is based on deception, in the case of Steve Barron. At the end she does receive a proposal from someone who knows the truth. Her refusal presumably signals an admirable embrace of penitence for past transgression.[1] As with many of Mulholland's novels a radical position is aired though the novel settles in the more conventional centre. Nonetheless, *Nanno* represents a more complex exploration than several other of her novels written around the same time. In *Onora* (1900) a servant girl ends her relationship with a young man as it would imperil the position of his family were he to marry her instead of a rich girl who has returned from America. *The Tragedy of Chris* (1903) is a straightforward contrast between the choices even poor women make between vice and respectability.[2]

Also noteworthy is the fact that Nanno receives counsel from a man, a priest. In *Marcella Grace* Marcella decides to perjure herself in order to help Bryan at this trial, until he dissuades her. In this regard Mulholland's worldview seems to reverse what is usually thought of as the Victorian notion that women, guardians of home and children, provide the moral guidance to men who must venture into the temptations of the world.

CHAPTER FIFTEEN

The news that Steve Barron was engaged to be married to the stranger who had arrived in the country only two months ago without a friend to speak for her, caused a sensation in the little world around Clonvallagh and Ardmore. From Father M'Carthy

---

1. Murphy, *Catholic Fiction*, pp. 32–3.
2. Murphy, *Catholic Fiction*, pp. 31–2.

in his parochial cottage under the chapel walls to the most insignificant squatter on the land, everyone had a word to say on the burning subject. Seldom do Irish farmers make such reckless marriages, and it was whispered in some quarters that Steve was bewitched. True, the girl was good-looking, but there were plenty of pretty and penniless girls throughout Waterford, and they were not invited to become the wives of farmers. It must be admitted that Barron was a bit of a stranger himself, and maybe he had brought home some new ways with him, However, it had been thought that he was going to make a man of himself, out and out, by a marriage with the heiress, Mary Cassidy. And where would he get, fortune or no forture, a better or a prettier girl than Mary? asked the gossips indignantly.

In the Cassidys' house only a few words on the subject were spoken. The look in Mary's face forbade more. After a week's silence the mother prepared to pay a visit to Father M'Carthy. She put on her best gown, and a large black bonnet over her white-frilled cap. Since Mary had been at school with the nuns, Mrs. Cassidy had never worn her large, deep-caped cloak in the old way with the hood over the head, but disposed it on her shoulders as cloaks are worn in towns. She took a clean-folded handkerchief and held it in her hands as she was used to do going to Mass on Sundays, and as she was leaving the house she reached for her prayer-book from a shelf, clasping it in front of her waist along with the handkerchief.

"Where are you goin' with this?" said Mary, taking it from her hands gently.

"Oh, now, didn't I think it was Mass I was goin'!" said Mrs. Cassidy, smiling nervously.

"Where is it that you are goin', mother?"

"Oh, just across to Father M'Carthy, to ask him to pray for your poor father. I've dreamt about him these two nights past, and it's maybe the good prayers that he is wantin'."

"Don't say too much, even to Father M'Carthy, mother," said

Mary. "My father had a bit of pride of his own, and remember your daughter's a Cassidy."

"Tut, child! Do you think your mother has no pride although she's only connected with the Cassidys?" retorted the widow, was a faint attempt at laughter. And then Mary retreated into the house, and Mrs. Cassidy departed on her errand to Father M'Carthy.

The Father was reading his breviary by such light as got into his little parlour through a window half smothered in ivy.

"Well now, Mrs. Cassidy, this is very good of you," said the old man, shaking her hand heartily, and pretending not to see the lines of pain in the woman's face—a strong face, in which sorrow took the colour of tragedy.

"I came to speak to you about Mary, Father," faltered the mother. "She'd be wild if she knew it, but your reverence is the only creature I can open my heart to."

"I know what you mean. It's about this business of Steve Barron," said the old priest.

"What in under the heavens is it all about?" said Mrs. Cassidy. "Is it true that he's goin' to marry that bit of a servant-girl that's been workin' above in the fields?"

"I'm afraid it is; I'm afraid it is," said Father M"Carthy. "I'm disappointed in Steve, I acknowledge it. I baptized him and Mary, and wanted to have married them. I went to him as soon as I heard of this, and, said he, 'I'm sorry to have vexed you, Father,' said he; 'but in the matter of a wife, you see, a man has to make a bold choice.'"

"We thought he had chose; me and Mary thought he had chose," said Mrs. Cassidy, rocking herself. "He looked it, and he acted it, Father; and Mary believed in him the same as if he had put words to it. She won't allow it now, scarcely even to her own mother, but I'm frightened at her more than if she was talkin' about it."

"Why, now Mrs. Cassidy," said the priest, smiling, "isn't there a good round dozen of excellent fellows this minute about the country just dying for your daughter to give them a look over her shoulder?"

"She won't look," said Mrs. Cassidy. "Mary's not one of the sort that will change her lovers like a hat or a jacket. She wasn't for marryin' at all, at all, till your reverence walked into the house that day with Steve to us, in the beginning of spring was a year. She was always for the convent, with a little sigh and a smile to herself, when she'd tell me of the heavenliness of the life the nuns do have. And it's off to the convent she wants to go now. Only for a retreat she says, but God knows I have a guess o' what her retreatin' will come to. And the look in her face eats into my very heart, Father. I could massacre myself to give her up to the Almighty, if He wanted her. I could sit down and be lonesome to the end of my days, in penance for my sins, but it's the look in her eyes that does knock me over entirely, Father M'Carthy, entirely. Them are no eyes to go into a convent an' be a nun with, I do keep sayin' to myself."

Mrs. Cassidy stopped and wept, and Father M'Carthy drew a step nearer to her.

Presently he said, "Well, now, my good friend, Mary's not going to be a nun unless she's wanted. Do you think the Sisters would have her unless she went cheerfully? You let her go and let her make her retreat. It'll help her over the awkwardness, and she'll come back to you content."

After a little homely spiritual counsel from her pastor, the sorrowful woman followed his suggestion and made an act of resignation to the will of God. The old man gave her his blessing and promised her his prayers, and she departed, trying to believe herself comforted.

She had not gone far on her journey before she met Moll Hurley, dressed in her Sunday best, and with her child in her arms.

"I was coming up to see you, Mrs. Cassidy. What's all this talk about my brother Stephen?"

In an instant, Mrs. Cassidy was another woman.

"I really don't know, Mrs. Hurley," she said, carelessly. "We did hear something about your brother goin' to be married."

Mrs. Hurley looked bitterly vexed. "Mrs. Cassidy," she said, "do you mean to tell me that your Mary has gone and refused Steve Barron?"

Mary's mother laughed. "Now, Moll," she said, "how can a girl like Mary be blamed for not marryin' everybody? It isn't every girl in the country has both money and looks. But Mary would kill me if she heard me talkin' this way. The truth is, I'm afraid it's a nun she's goin' to be on me. There's nothing in her head but makin' a retreat this long while back. I suppose I'll have to give my consent and let me off with her."

But Moll was not appeased. "They do say she gave great encouragement to Steve a short while ago, and he never would have done what he's doin' if your Mary hadn't jilted him," she hurled forth resentfully.

Mrs. Cassidy saw her advantage, and made the most of her opportunity for a quarrel. It would be too much to have Moll Hurley paying visits to Mary at such a crisis.

"Steve's a good fellow," she said patronizingly, "but I think you make a little too much fuss about him, Mrs. Hurley. I daresay the girl he is going to marry will answer him finely. There isn't a Mary of my sort for every man that's goin'."

"Make too much fuss about him! Every man that's goin'!" Moll stared and stammered before she could articulate a syllable.

"No one ever heard of such language used about Steve Barron before, Mrs. Cassidy," she said, angrily.

"I used no language. Every bit of language that was used came from yourself, Mrs. Hurley," returned Mrs. Cassidy, with dignity, upon which Moll, exasperated beyond the possibility for further speech, turned abruptly, and walked away rapidly.

Thus it got about that Mary had refused Steve Barron, and that his attachment to Nanno was love caught at the rebound. Under cover of this suggestion, Mary got away to the convent, and the mother held the fort of her child's pride against all comers, for it was the moment when gossip walked the country from house to house, and as was natural, came more frequently to Mrs. Cassidy's door than to any other. Meanwhile, Steve was too much preoccupied with his happiness to be aware of what was being said about him. Even to his sister he turned but half an ear, answered reproaches with the utmost good humour, and forgot what she said to him before he was out of her presence.

There was a pause in the field work. Nanno stayed within doors, knitting and sewing with Bridget and Ellen O'Daly. In the evenings, Steve came down through the green boreens leading from the slopes and fields of the farm, to the cottage at the back of the sea-cliff, under the shadow of St Declan's big round tower and the shattered arches of the ruined monastery.

CHAPTER SIXTEEN

Steve and Nanno were among the ruins on the huge shoulder of the cliffs overlooking the sea and Ardmore. As they sat on a broken cross beside St Declan's oratory they could see, looking down, Ellen O'Daly sitting on her doorstep in the saffron light of after-sunset, and could hear snatches of her song carried to them when the breeze blew their way.

Sometimes they stopped their lovers' talk for a minute to listen to the singing. Steve was pressing for an early day for their marriage. Nanno besought him for a longer delay. She knew she must go to Dublin alone before the wedding, and either bring the child back with her, or, at least, place it somewhere outside the poorhouse walls. To bring it to Ardmore at once would be the safest course. Meanwhile, she was in no hurry for interruption of her present extraordinary new-found happiness as Stephen's promised wife.

Ellen and Bridget and she had been up to Steve's house to spend an evening. Moll Hurley had been asked to come to entertain them, but was too indignant to respond, and so the three young women had managed to do without her. Steve had made all the little preparations that a man could think of, and Nanno had poured out the tea and Bridget had toasted cakes. Steve took them over the house and farm, and Nanno was shown the new dairy that Moll had built, and the rooms both upstairs and downstairs. Here was the room where his mother had slept, and this little nook was Steve's own den when he was a boy. He had brought back some of the old time-honoured furniture from a neighbour, and there was his mother's old store-press, and her pin-cushion, and the holy water font that used to hand above her bed, and her crucifix. As Steve stood with Nanno before these simple and sacred relics, he stole and arm round her shoulder and drew her face up to his own; and to the girl who had so late been an outcast his kiss had the solemnity of a sacrament. Though she could not have described it so, she felt it like a baptism. Before leaving the place, while Bridget and Helen waited outside the threshold, she had stood a few minutes on the kitchen hearth with her hand in Steve's. It was the supreme hour of her life. She felt keenly that the precious things she had coveted were hers, the honoured home, the safe and happy surroundings, and above and beyond all this great thing she had never dreamed of, the love and unquestioning confidence of a good and tender man. Even her anguish in the possession of her child and her worship of him had scarcely any existence for her in this inexpressible moment.

But as usual there had been the reaction. That night she lay down to sleep exulting. Truly had she kept her word when she vowed that she would make herself respectable. If the girls in the poorhouse could only know all that she had risen to! But the pride of this thought gave place to her agony, as by the light of her new experience she saw her past transgressions. That lying paper by which she fought her way upward, must be taken back to Dublin and shown to Father Shannon.

Those falsehoods she had told about the husband who was

dead? She could never unsay them, and must now only try never to think of them. It was a little relief to her to remember that Steve had come to the conclusion that the imaginary husband had been unkind to her, and would accept this as a reason for her unwillingness to talk about him. After a feverish night, face to face with her sins, she arose, braced to something of her old irresponsible daring. She would be good for the future, but she must not be too grieved about the past. Why need anything matter, after all, since Steve loved her and had promised to be a father to the child? She would see her little lad playing in the fields and holding up his head with the best of them. The only thing worth striving for now was to keep her lover in his present state of ignorance with regard to her unhappy antecedents.

She was still in this mood while she sat with Barron on the hill of the ruins, and heard the snatches of Ellen O'Daly's singing between the extravagances of his love-making. All at once Steve began to make a new proposal which filled her with fear.

"Now, Nanno," he said, "what's to hinder our being married at once and going off together to bring home the child?"

Nanno was silent a moment from sheer terror; then she said:

"It wouldn't do at all. I want to go to Dublin first and get a few little things for myself. I can then bring back the child, and Ellen will take care of him for me till you want him home."

"Couldn't you get what you require in Youghal? I think it would be far nicer for the pair of us to take a trip to Dublin after we're married," urged Steve. Nanno rapidly considered the situation.

"Of course we can do that if you like." she said; "but I must go first myself to make arrangements. I'll need to see the person the child is with; but I won't bring him back with me this time if you object to it."

Steve said no more, surprised at the anxiety expressed in her face. He put it down to her pride of independence, which appeared to him the one obstinate trait in her character.

"Well, dear, do as you please," he said, with the air of a bewitched man, as he watched the breeze twisting the wreaths of her fair hair into a tangle of gold above her forehead. "But if you're not in a hurry to go, and won't marry me before you go, it's puttin' things off a long way ahead, my darlin'."

"I'm happy enough with the way I am," said Nanno.

"I'm not, though—I want to be happier. And another thing is this. How are you to live in the meantime while you're dilly-dallying? I don't like to have my promised wife goin' workin' about the fields; and you're too proud in yourself to take money from me."

"Will Cruise is very good to me," said Nanno. "he gets me a little money for mendin' the nets."

Steve frowned. "I can't have you takin' money from the like of Will Cruise," he said.

"There isn't the like of him," said Nanno; "not for kindness."

"He's a good enough fellow," said Steve discontentedly. "I tell you what it is, Nanno; I'll find out where the child is staying, and I'll go for him without you. That is what I'll do if you don't hurry yourself."

Nanno turned a pair of scared eyes on him; but he had looked away from her after a bat that had whirred past them out of the ruin, and he did not see her glance. Before his eyes has come back from their momentary wandering, she had righted herself.

"You can go if you like," she said, saucily, "but maybe you won't find me here when you come back."

"What time will you go, Nanno?"

"Will Monday suit you?"

"This is Friday. Couldn't you get away sooner?"

"I'll go on Monday."

"How long will it take you to do the business and come back?"

"I'll be back by Thursday."

And so it was settled. Nanno had kept some of Father Tom's money put away in the old purse he had given her, so that she might never be without means of going back to the child. Added to this savings, enough to repay Father Tom's loan, though she knew what he had given her was meant as a present, also something over to buy clothes to replace her darling's pauper garb. She set out on her journey without accepting money pressed on her by Steve, and in return for many concessions on his part she allowed him to accompany her as far as Cork, and to put her in the train to Dublin.

CHAPTER SEVENTEEN

So suspicious and fearful was Nanno, that, hurrying along Dublin streets, she often turned her head to assure herself that Steve was not following her. She was haunted by the dread that he had some misgiving about her, and might have got on the train at the last moment for the purpose of watching her, and she only felt at ease on the point when, having keenly surveyed all the approaches to the poorhouse before entering, she heard the clang of the old familiar gates closing behind her.

Nanno, with bright, healthy looks and neat dress, was so changed that at first no one recognized her, and she was taken for a respectable visitor come to see one of the paupers. No sooner, however, was her errand made known that the news went round among such of her old companions as were in the place that Nanno Breen had come back like a lady, and was asking about her child. A number of girls collected in the yard to interview her, but in the meantime Nanno had escaped them and made her way to "The Infants'."

Her heart beat fast as the door of the Infant School opened, and she was again in the room where her earliest childhood had been passed, and face to face with the little old woman who had been her first tutoress. Some people said that Miss Finality's name was an assumed one, and that the woman herself had belonged to a class above her present position. However, that might be, she had held her post here for forty years, and grown portly and dignified at her occupation. She has an air of comfortableness in her old age which was striking as compared with the listless depression of rows of human mites on the benches before her. The fresh russet tint of her cheeks was in contrast with her lips, slightly fallen in from loss of teeth, the whiteness of her hair, and the long wrinkles across her puckered forehead. She wore a black-bordered cap, tied under her chin, a black gown and silk mantle of a bygone fashion, heavily trimmed with velvet and fringe of a blackness well bronzed with the rust of time.

Nanno's brilliant face, with shining eyes, and a bright carnation in her cheeks, was quite unrecognized by the old lady till the girl spoke.

"Oh, Miss Finality, don't you know me? I'm Nanno Breen, and I'm come for my boy. Where is he?"

"Nanno Breen!" Miss Finality rubbed her spectacles and put them on, but while she was doing so, the mother had already found her boy, and snatched him from among the children, who sat in the benches raised one above another against the wall.

"My Jim! My Jim! don't you know Mammy?" she cried, with something between a wail and a laugh.

The little fellow made a wry mouth, and beat his face away with his open hands, struggled out of her arms, and ran to Miss Finality. Nanno dropped down on a bench, and put her head on her knees, and burst into wild sobbing and weeping. The old woman came and stood beside her, and patted her on the shoulder.

"Nanno, Nanno! Now I know you. Such a girl as you always were for getting into a storm! Give the poor baby time. How can he remember you when even myself that had you and your mother both at his age didn't recognise you. Come here now, Jim, and look at pretty, pretty mammy."

The old lady took the child on her knee and sat on the bench beside Nanno.

"He's beginning to remember," she went on. "Tell me all about yourself in the meantime. I hope you have been doing well, my girl."

"The best of well, ma'am," said Nanno. She had dried up her tears, and sat gazing with rapture at the little curly head and blossom-like face which were so like her own. "I got way to the country Miss Finality, and I've lived a good life with respectable people. Nobody knows anything against me, where I've been. And if anybody ever comes asking about me here, you won't tell stories of me, will you Miss Finality?"

"Indeed I won't, my dear. God knows. I'd be glad to part with the tongue out of my head if all the girls I ever reared could give me the same account of themselves."

"I won't tell you where I live now, ma'am, for fear someone would pick it out of you some time or other," said Nanno, her eyes fixed on her child's eyes, which stared at her with fascination, as if Nature were persuading him that here was his mother, and he had already given half an ear to her.

"But, oh, Miss Finality, it is sweet and good to be among the country folks. They're all so decent, and such behavior with them; and they say their prayers; and even the smell of the turf burning would very nearly put a crooked body straight."

"It is true, it is true," said the old lady, taking off her spectacles to wipe her eyes.

"And, Miss Finality, I was taught to say my prayers while I was here, but I never had the heart for them till I went and saw the people in their homes. I'm only an ignorant girl, ma'am, but will you tell me why people that pay for rearing us here, shut us up in a hell of a house like this, instead of putting us out some place where we'd have a chance of gettin' on the ways of an innocent life?"

"I don't know, dear, I don't know. It's a matter that has always puzzled me. I wish I had a chance to speak my mind in public. But I'm too old, Nanno, and nobody would listen to me. Someday, perhaps, the world will waken up to see the horror of keeping a nursery for evil in the State. But it won't be in my day. I hope it may be in yours."

My boy will be out of it, anyhow, Miss Finality, and I trust that myself will never be tracked. Oh, see, ma'am, he's holdin' out his hands to me. Jim, Jim, look at the pretty frock that poor mammy has brought for you!"

The child was coaxed into allowing himself to be undressed and dressed again, and at last, all formalities under authority having been gone through, Nanno said goodbye to Miss Finality, and carried him off with her.

In the yard she had to pass through groups of her old acquaintances who had assembled to see her go out, and have a word with her. She spoke to some and nodded to others, but said nothing to anyone of her circumstances or new ways of life. This passage was a trial, but she bore it with fortitude, and left it behind her as she escaped into the outer precincts of the poorhouse.

As the gates of the hated asylum were opened to let her go out, a man passed in who looked at her with recognition and surprise. For a moment he appeared as if he would speak to her, but seeing that she was absorbed with the boy, stooping down to coax him to walk with her, he did not arrest her attention, but went on into the Union premises, while mother and child were in the act of quitting them.[3]

Once outside the gates Nanno took the child in her arms and ran without stopping as long as she was able. When quite out of breath and dizzy from sustained effort, she set the boy on his feet, put her hands to her panting sides, and looked around her. She was far out of sight of the poorhouse walls now; no one meeting her with her child could form any idea of where they had come from. Exulting in this final severance from her hated antecedents, she went on with light steps in the direction of SS. Matthew and Luke.

Going straight to the parochial dwelling house, she knocked boldly, and asked to be admitted to see Father Shannon. He was

---

3. An administrative body called the Poor Law Union ran the workhouses.

in his room, said the housekeeper, with a sigh for the Father's short moments of leisure gone. Nanno was shown into a sparsely-furnished parlour, suggestive of vestry-meetings. How happily different was this from her last visit here, thought Nanno, as she carried her boy round the room and showed him the saints and martyrs framed on the wall, and her own face and the child's smiling in the glass of the pictures. Then the door opened, and she saw the well-remembered spare figure in worn black gown and rusty biretta come with a rapid movement into the room.

"No, my child; I don't know you," said Father Tom, turning on her is soft, dark, short-sighted eyes, luminous in the pallor of a face which was pathetic in its expression of infinite patience and sweetness.

"I'm glad you don't, Father," said Nanno; "and I don't know myself, neither. But maybe you'll remember the girl you gave a handful of money to a few months ago. You trusted me Father, and your blessing has thruv' with me."

"I know you now," said Father Shannon, throwing back his head, and looking at her in astonishment. "And you're sure that this is you?" he added, smiling radiant approval, "in spite of appearances?"

"I think it's me; I think it's me," said Nanno, with a flashing tear, "though nobody recognizes me, no more than myself, not even the boy here, that I've taken to-day *out of where he was*, Father," lowering her voice as if afraid that even the saints in the pictures on the walls might overhear the allusion to the poorhouse.

"Ah, yes; the boy. And where in the world have you been working your miracles, my poor child? for never in all my life did I see such a transformation, thank God!" said the Father, striving to find traces in the bright, blooming young woman before him of a sullen, defiant face, a shrinking and miserably-clad figure.

"On the Waterford farms, Father. I told you I wanted to get into the country and to work in the fields, and I got what I wanted. I've earned for myself, and I've kept myself respectable. Sure, there's goodness in the very winds that's blowin' over them parts, Father, and nobody there knows but I'm as good as the best of them."

"And so you are, my child, and so you are and will be. Good girl, good girl, to come back and tell me."

"There's more than that I have to tell. "I did a very bad thing, Father, though it was the first of my good fortune. And I can't rest easy in my mind till I have your forgiveness for it."

"What did you do?" he asked in a grave, low tone. "Don't be afraid of me. What is the very worst thing that you did, poor child, since I saw you."

Nanno was fumbling in her pocket, and now produced that paper on which Father Shannon had written his signature. She unfolded it with nervous fingers, and gave it open into his hands.

"I see. A forgery. Oh, my God!"

He dropped the paper, which fluttered to the floor, and covered his eyes with his hand.

"Why, why did you commit this crime?"

Nanno's lips became white, and she put her hand to the table to support herself. She had known she done very wrong in this matter, but had not realised that the Father, who was all charity, would call her action a crime.

"I wanted a character, Father. I couldn't get on without it. I knew I was going to act honest. Hardly anybody saw it, but just the name of it helped me–"

"Why could you not have asked me to write something for you?"

"You didn't know me, Father, and I never thought of it till after I was gone from you."

Father Tom stooped and picked up the paper from the floor and tore it across and across.

"It is gone," he said; "blotted out. You can never be accused of it now. Promise me, on your soul, on your hope of heaven, never to do anything of the kind in all your life again."

"I do promise," said Nanno. "I don't want to do it. And what's more, Father I'll never have need to do it again. I've brought you back the money that you lent me. There's something else that I have to tell you, but all of it's good. I'm not the same as I was, Father. I've begun to say my prayers, and to love God in earnest; and what I want is to till you how it happened to me."

Then, with rapid changing colour, in hurried sentences, with breathless pauses, and now and then a burst of tears, Nanno told of Steve's manly wooing, and of the happy and honourable life that lay before her, and the Father was made to understand that it was the sacred wifely love aroused in her heart that had wrought a thorough conversation in her.

"And there's nothin' he won't do for me, Father. He'll take the child and make his own of him. And I'll have the best of a home. If you saw the fields of it, Father, and the trees, and the beasts rovin' about, and the birds singin', and all the good neighbours goin' in and out and thinkin' well of you. An' I'll try to be as good as his mother was—there's her crucifix on the wall, and her old, prayer book. Steve keeps them, and, O Father, it's easy to be good when a man like Steve Barron's got his heart on you."

A grave trouble had gathered in Father Tom's eyes, and as Nanno's voice with its passionate tenderness, wavered into silence he did not answer immediately.

"Does this man, this trusting man, know the whole of your story, my poor, poor child?" he said, in tones of infinite pity and sympathy.

Nanno started, and colour and light ebbed away out of her cheeks and eyes, and she turned a dumb look on Father Tom, such as some helpless animal might turn on one whose caressing hand had suddenly pierced it with a murderous knife.

Father Tom silently waited for her reply. Twice she made an effort to speak, but her white lips failed to form the words, and she desisted.

"Does he know?" repeated Father Tom, with exquisite gentleness.

"He does not know," burst forth Nanno, in a vehement half whisper. "How would he know, Father? It's what I'm trying to manage that he never know. He thinks I'm just the same as the best of the good girls that he sees there around him. He believes that I had a sailor husband, an' he died away at sea; and I've thought that much over the story myself that I've nearly come to believe it's the truth o' what happened to me. We're cut off from the poorhouse, me an' the child, now, and Waterford's a long way off from here, and the people don't be travellin', and Steve himself has never a call come to Dublin—"

Father Tom sat silent and pondering. The deepest depths of feeling in the man's nature threw up their shadows now, and drew lines of tragedy in a face expressive of intensity of sympathy with the unassuageable sorrows of humanity.

"I do not see how you can marry him, my poor child, without letting him know." Nanno's face was white now, and her body began to shiver. Dropping on her knees at the Father's feet, she put her trembling hands together as a child does who says its prayers, and made appeal to him.

"Father, I couldn't tell him. He couldn't help hatin' an' scornin' me, and how could I make him understand the way things happened to me? It wasn't my own choice. If I'd been brought up in the fields an' the little homes, I would have been a woman like his mother from the first. But the poor-house gave me never a chance. You're kept in the school as *that* (pointing her trembling finger at the child), and just when you're old enough to come to harm, you're tossed out into the badness that's watchin' for you. If Steve knew it all as I know it, he'd forgive me, but I'm full sure that he never could be happy with me. If my body was dead an' buried, and it was only my soul that was to live with him, he might forget it, but I've learnt all the differ by the love that he's put in me. I heard the story of Mary Magdalen, Father, but I never rightly took it in. She knew she was unhappy, and she knew she was ill-treated, but she never rightly knew what she was till the Lord turned His eyes on her. *He* knew it all because He was God—but Steve isn't God, though I think he comes very near to Him—"

She stopped breathless, and bent her head nearer the ground, shaking with the passion of her terror and anguish. The child, who had been playing with his hat on the floor, toddled towards her, crying out, "Mammy, mammy, get up out of that!" and the mother folded her arms about him and held him tightly to her, and the touch of him seemed to quiet her.

"I did not say you ought to tell him." began Father Tom, pitifully, his eyes dim with tears, his voice husky with pain. "I think it is very likely that he could not get over it. But, my child, under the circumstances, ought you to marry him?"

Nanno ceased rocking the child, and let him slip out of her arms, which fell limp by her sides as if no more able to support themselves.

"I promised to marry him," she said; "he loves me, and he will not take any answer but the one. A month ago I did not care; I wanted only to keep out of his way. But I opened my heart to it, and I cannot go back. The very smile of him is like the goodness of God to me, and I cannot give it up. Even the child there that was all my life isn't as much to me as Steve is now."

"I know it, my poor child, I know it," said Father Tom. "It is a terrible strait that you are in, a fiery trial you have to bear. But I am thinking of the good man's trust—and of the future of you both in case——"

The last two or three words fell on ears that did not hear, for Nanno suddenly pitched sideways from her knees to the floor and lay there unconscious.

Father Tom brought water from a table and wet her face and hands, tears running from his eyes as he did so. He eased her position and placed her head level with her body on the floor, and bathed her forehead again, and at last Nanno came back with a long sigh, back from the quiet of death, and was at first aware only of her heart in pain, but soon became conscious again of sorrow and struggle that caused its intolerable ache. With the help of Father Tom's hand she managed to rise to her feet, and sat limp and silent on a bench, waiting for strength to get up and walk out of the presence of the gentle friend who had unexpectedly turned so cruel.

Father Tom had slipped away to beg a cup of tea from the housekeeper, who was not always sympathetic to such occasions. "They do break his heart with their stories," she would grumble, "and when they have got all they wants they go off laughing, the half of them."

However, this time she was amenable, having felt a little surprised joy at the flower-faces of mother and child as they passed through the door, reminding her of the fields and of her girlhood.

Nanno swallowed the tea eagerly, with a grateful look at the giver. It is not certain that she had ever heard the story of Francis and the lepers,[4] but she felt all their wonder and love at being served in her humiliation by a saint, none the less because her heart was stubborn and rebellious under her gratitude. She gave the empty cup back into his hands silently, and began putting on her hat and gathering up the child in her arms, who poor mite, had fallen asleep with his head in the folds of her gown at her feet.

Father Tom picked up her little mantle and put it on her shoulders, with the air of a penitent brother who had grievously wounded his sister. When she was quite ready to go, he said, sorrowfully:

"I don't want to hurt you again, my child, but let me say a few more words. I will not take the responsibility of advising you in this matter. I believe I am right in the view I take, but I would make an appeal from my judgement. I would counsel you lay the case before a wiser mind than mine. You know the Church of Saint Bridgid on the other side of the river? Will you go there and find out Father Benedict of the Order of Mount Olivet?[5] You will

---

4. St Francis of Assisi (1181–1226) nursed lepers at one stage in his career.
5. The Olivetians are a branch of the Order of Saint Benedict.

see his name on the confessional in Saint Bridgid's. He has more experience in the confessional, more knowledge of the ways of the human heart, my poor child, than any man I ever knew. Go to him and tell him your story as you told it to me. I am satisfied to let you abide by his judgement."

Nanno gazed at Father Tom, fascinated by his humility and tenderness, and she answered mechanically, "I will go, Father." Then he showed her into the hall as if she had been a great lady, and, himself, closed the door behind her when she had passed, with his final blessing, into the street.

Still sick and weak, Nanno took her way across one of the river bridges in the direction of the Church of Saint Bridgid, walking slowly under the weight of the sleeping child, all thought paralysed, her mind lost in a shapeless dream of pain. As the air stirred about her head and roused her senses a little, she began to feel the touch of the child's warm cheek nestling on her neck, and she grew aware that the burden she carried was sweet, and the joy of nature gradually awoke in her. After all, Father Tom had not decided against her. This other priest might hold a different opinion. Hope sprang in her heart again, and the colour of life flowed back into her lips and cheeks. Her steps grew lighter and quicker, and when the church was found she almost ran up the steps in her eagerness to hear the words which would order her back to happiness.

It was the eve of a holiday, and there were a good many people in the church. The confessionals were surrounded, and Nanno noticed, with a feeling of relief, contradictory of her mood of a few minutes go, that some time must elapse before she could whisper her appeal to Father Benedict. The church was a dark one, but from a high window light fell on his confessional. Having prayed long with only half-articulated passion, she got up from her knees and sat gazing now at the altar half hid in shadow, and now at the lettering above the confessional. In a few more minutes in would be her turn to seek counsel of Father Benedict.

What would he answer to her? In her anxiety she was beginning to forget all the moving words she had thought of speaking to him. She felt the power the power of stating her case to be passing away from her, and a dumb, helpless conviction that she was hopelessly condemned gathered in a cloud over her brain. Father Benedict would assuredly give his judgement against her. If Father Shannon, who was all pity, had felt obliged to do so, how could it be otherwise with this new, and perhaps less merciful judge? These men of God were cruel. The God whose mouthpiece they were must be cruel. Steve, and Steve only, was good.

Having arrived at this conclusion, Nanno was seized with a supernatural terror. If a second voice were to condemn her, then this fear of a spiritual verdict against her would be too much for her, and she would have to give way. She could never see Steve's face again—never return to Waterford. The old familiar horror of the river returned, and she saw at once Steve's eyes watching for her at the railway station, and herself and the child lying stark at the bottom of the mud-water. The instinct of life roused her from this hideous dream. She would go while there was yet time. She would not enter that confessional to hear her doom. The child was sleeping in her lap, and she took him up again in her arms, and knelt for a moment, mutely asking God to forgive and have mercy on her; and she left the church with the purpose of her coming unfulfilled.

She had intended staying the night in Dublin, and travelling by morning train. Steve was to meet her at the terminus at Cork. Now she resolved to depart from Dublin at once, lest a fatal impulse to consult Father Benedict should seize on her in the interval. Arrived in Cork too soon, she spent the early hours in the sense of having escaped a great danger. When the moment at last arrived, she took her place on the platform, and saw Steve watching for her before he caught sight of her. There was eager joyous expectation in his face. He stood out from among the other men on the platform, tall and square, with all his heart in his eyes, asking for its delight.

A few swift steps, and her touch was on his arm. Dublin, and all memory of its terrors and dangers were left behind like a forgotten nightmare. She was kissed tenderly and reverently, as well-loved wives are kissed; and Steve took the boy from her arms with a little glad laugh, and a quick glance from the babe's face to the woman's, and a flying thought of pity for the sailor husband at the bottom of the sea, who had lost his bliss, and left it to fall to the share of another.

6

The Return of Mary O'Murrough.
London and Edinburgh, Sands and Co., 1908.

Chapters Ten to Twelve

Introduction

Mrs. Dermody, a widow, has two daughters. When prosperous, elderly Pether Flynn offers to marry pretty Bess Dermody without a dowry, Mrs. Dermody decides to discourage Bess's connection with Miles Donohue. Shan Sullivan is engaged to Mary O'Murrough, but she has been in America for many years, making money so they can marry. Emigration is prevalent in the area. Bad blood grows between Flynn and Donohue. Bess, unable to marry Miles because of her mother's disapproval, herself considers emigration. Shan writes to Mary to return home but is arrested and charged with a cattle mutilation that he did not commit.[1]

In Chapter Ten Mary arrives home, but is so aged by her years abroad that no one initially recognizes her. In Chapter Eleven she lodges with the Dermodys and there is debate over whether the money she has made will be considered by Shan as a compensation for the loss of her good looks. In Chapter Twelve she goes to look after Shan's father and people get used to her appearance.

---

1. The mutilation of cattle was one of the tactics sometimes resorted to in Ireland by those with a grudge against the owner of the cattle.

She eventually visits Shan in jail and is upset when he does not recognize her. Meanwhile, the local priest, Fr Fahy, succeeds in proving that the crime Shan was charged with is a police setup, perhaps designed to discredit moves towards Home Rule, as domestic self-government for Ireland within the United Kingdom, to which Irish nationalists aspired, was known. Now released, Shan asks Mary to marry him, but she says she does not want to marry someone who no longer loves her. She decides to emigrate once more and to leave her money for Shan and anyone he might marry. However, Shan and Mary are themselves reconciled and get married. Bess and Miles marry but emigrate to America.

Though things end happily for Mary O'Murrough she spends most of the novel as the rejected woman. In this she resembles Brigid Lavelle in "The Hungry Death" and Mary Cassidy in *Nanno*. Most agonizing for Mary is the fact that the cause of her rejection is her lost good looks which have been sacrificed in her attempts to establish a proper economic basis for her marriage. Yet female attractiveness functions, albeit evanescently, as a form of capital in something of the same way as do the products of the land: like a perishable crop, beauty diminishes with age. That women's beauty is more a function of the male erotic imagination may to some extent explain the otherwise surreal reception Mulholland contrives for Mary on her return home. It is as if Shan's erotic imagination has been projected onto the entire population. No one at all recognises her. Even the story's happy ending is qualified. Female erotic attraction to heterosexual males is of course linked with fertility and fecundity. Mary duly becomes pregnant but the infant dies in childbirth and Mary and Shan remain infertile thereafter.

Seven years later in *Norah of Waterford* (1915), however, Mulholland reworked some of the themes of *The Return of Mary O'Murrough*. Both novels use a theme common in Mulholland, that of the returned emigrant or exile. Norah's dilemma is that of a poor young woman who wishes to marry. Her rival is a rich, older woman who has returned from America in search of a husband. However, whereas Mary O'Murrough was seen as virtuous and sympathetic, this woman is presented as grotesque and unsympathetic in her efforts to simulate a lost beauty in the hope of making herself marriageable by combining wealth with beauty. The novel ends with the older woman admitting defeat and acting as an advocate for Norah's marriage in the spirit of women's cooperation, albeit within the grim world of Irish rural economics and marriage. Both novels gesture towards the downward trajectory of what had once been Mulholland's progressive optimism concerning women, land and the positive role of the returned exile in Ireland, in novels such as *A Fair Emigrant* (1888).[2]

CHAPTER TEN
"I'M MARY O'MURROUGH FROM AMERICA."

The passengers by an American liner had been landed at Queenstown.[3] In the midst of the bustle, friends meeting, travellers hurrying to catch trains, hustling of porters and hauling of luggage, a young woman stood apart, searching the crowd with earnest eyes, eager to recognise someone who did not appear. After an hour's waiting she sat on her trunk still, an image of patience, until finding that she was attracting attention she shook off her air of intense expectation, and departed like her fellow-travellers for the railway station.

"To Ballyorglin?" said the porter. "We can't send you all the way, but you've just missed the train that would take you nearest to it."

---

2. James H. Murphy, "'She's nothin' but a shadda": The Politics of Marriage in Late Mulholland,' in Anna Pilz and Whitney Standlee (eds.), *Advancing the Cause of Liberty: Irish Women's Writing, 1878–1922* (Manchester, Manchester University Press, 2016), pp. 33–48; Hansson, 'Returning Exile,' p. 100.
3. Queenstown, formerly Cove, now Cobh, is a seaport in County Cork. Passenger ships departed and arrived there from America.

"I'm a long time out of this," said the woman. "I thought you might have a train to it by now."

She retired to the waiting-room, on her face still that look of enduring patience, her whole person indicating by movement and non-movement a steadfast energy of character. Her dress was neat and plain, the black hat shaded a thin worn countenance. After half-an-hour's perfect quietude she left the waiting-room and walked up and down the platform, decision in her step, and some pride in the carriage of her head and shoulders.

Arrived at her station she hired a car, and was driven the seven or eight miles which had to be travelled still to reach Ballyorglin, gazing intently at one point after another of the landscape, the joy of recognition still overshadowed by that failure of someone who had been counted on to meet her.

The carman took her to a little inn, where she was received by a blooming young woman with a baby in her arms. It was now dark, and an oil lamp was burning in the small parlour of the house of entertainment.

"Y'll never get on to Killelagh tonight," said the mistress of the place. "We can give y' a bed an' a cup o' tea. How far are y' afther comin', if I may be askin'?"

"I came from Queenstown to-day," said the stranger. "I've come from America, too, but that took me eight or nine days."

"So it would. An' ye've come over to see Ireland? Maybe yer father an' mother was Irish?"

"They were," said the stranger, gratefully accepting the tea set before her by her hostess. "How are the people up there in Killelagh?"

"They're well enough, all that's left o' them. A power o' them's emigratin' ivery month or so. An' it's that brings the sorra; to them that's stayin' as well as them that's goin'."

"Father Fahy is still the priest up there, I believe?"

"Of course he is. Sure Killelagh widout Father Fahy would be like a face widout eyes. Isn't he the comfort in everythin'? Look at him the other day when Shan Sullivan was took—"

"Took where?"

"To jail by the pólis. Mother in heaven, girl, what's the matther wid y'? Yer gone as white as my apron!"

"I'm tired," said the stranger. "What did Shan Sullivan do?"

"Nothin'. Put down for an act that he niver done. The case was made out dead against him. There was no witnesses but the pólis, an' his own word was not to be taken. So there he is. Maybe yer father an' mother knew his people."

"They did," said the stranger faintly.

"An' who might you be now? I suppose it's no harm to ask, an' you comin' to see us."

"My name is Mary O'Murrough."

"Mary O'Murrough! Maybe you're some relation to Shan's sweetheart that went to America, an' was always comin' home, an' isn't come yet?"

"I am," said the stranger.

"See that now, how well I guessed it. Maybe yer an aunt of hers, though I niver heard she had anyone there before her. She wasn't a bit like you, anyway, except that you have somethin' of the blue in the eyes. Oh, sure, Mary an' me were comrades at school, an' she was the purtiest crature y' could clap your eyes on. Did y' ever see the blue on the side o' Mangerton?[4] That was her eyes. An' her lips was as red as the holly berries at Christmas, an' her cheeks were as smooth as milk, an' two dimples in them!"

"But sure yer dead bet wid the journey, an' y'd betther get to your bed."

Next morning Mary O'Murrough left her trunk at the inn to be called for, and with a small bundle in her hand set out to walk to Killelagh. The sad look on her face deepened when she found herself alone on the road, every turn of which was familiar to her memory. Shan's failure to keep his promise to meet her at the boat, and the reason for it, had been a hard blow followed by

---

4. A mountain in County Kerry.

one harder still, and the words "she wasn't a bit like you" had left a sting of their own in her ears. There was little change in her school-fellow, the woman at the inn, and Mary had shrunk from revealing her own identity, not having before thoroughly realised the change that had been wrought in her own personal appearance. Overwhelmed by keen anxiety for Shan's unhappy state, and a new dread that he, too, if he saw her, would not recognise her, she struggled with a sense of more entire forlornness than had ever been experienced by her when the ocean had separated her from her old home and kindred. But this was soon controlled, and aided by a habit of courage she gathered up her energy, and her bundle, and proceeded on her journey.

Arrived at Killelagh, she looked eagerly around. There were the long hills in their winter grey, and the big mountain crags behind them. Here, the green pastures, and the little hedged fields. A gleam of cold sunlight touched the streams now full and moving, and shone in the pools of the brown bog that are like open eyes looking up to heaven. Over yonder were the homes, among them the ruined walls of the house in which she had been born. Further away was Shan Sullivan's farm. The house was not visible, but she knew the clump of trees that hid it from her view.

The chapel with its cross was a striking feature of the landscape; close to it the cottage of the priest, with its roof of thatch.

"Thank God for Father Fahy! I will go to him first!" was her conclusion after a wide look around the scene, so familiar, yet from which she had been so long estranged. The fact that Shan was not there, and the reason why, after years of separation, he could not receive her with joy, seemed to set her still further aloof from friends, to deny her any welcome from the well-remembered homes of Killelagh.

The priest's door was always open, a home to all; and with a vivid recollection of a kind face bending over her dying mother, Mary O'Murrough hastened her steps to Father Fahy's little garden wicket.

The Father was just leaving his house as she approached, and met her appealing look with—

"Well, my child, is there anything I can do for you?"

"Father Fahy! Do you not remember me?"

The old man adjusted his spectacles on his nose and looked at her attentively:

"I do not, child. Ought I to know you? Did I ever set eyes on you before?"

"You did, Father. You christened me. And you buried my mother. I'm Mary O'Murrough from America."

"God bless my soul! Mary O'Murrough! But—but—I remember Mary well, and you—and you——"

"I know, Father! I'm changed. It's a good many years since I left home, and I worked hard, and went through trouble. I'm not the girl I was when I said good-bye to Killelagh."

The priest looked at her, astonished and compassionate.

"Well, my child, I'm sorry you've come at the present moment."

"Shan wrote for me, Father. He bid me come at once, and no more puttin' off."

"So he did—so he did. But something happened. I promised to write to keep you back a bit. And I wrote. But you started before the letter had time to reach you."

"I came as fast as I could come. I know why Shan didn't come to meet me as he said he would. I heard it in Ballyorglin."

"Come into the house till I talk to you." He brought her into his little parlour, and seated her at the fire in his own old timeworn leather-lined arm-chair.

"Now, Mary O'Murrough, my poor child, you'll have to keep up your heart. You know where Shan is to spend his Christmas?"

"He's in the County Jail, Father. It must have been villainy that put him there. Shan would do nothin' to earn it."

"Of course there was villainy. But who did the deed is the mystery. Shan went into the field to look after Rorke's cattle when he heard them moaning, and guessed there was something wrong; and the police found him there, and arrested him for maiming the animals. He was brought before the magistrate at once, the assizes came on in a day or two afterwards, and the case was made out against him, black enough. His father and Rorke had been quarrelling about a bit of land, and Shan had been taken alone in the field with the cattle, and blood on his hands. So they made short work of him, so they did, my poor child; but God'll put it right for us yet. Never fear but the Almighty will make little of their circumstantial evidence!"

Mary's face drooped, and two or three heavy tears fell on her clasped hands. But she lifted her head again in half a minute.

"How long will they keep him in prison, Father?"

"Three years is the term, my child—but——"

The Father broke down. What comfort was meant to follow his "but" did not appear.

"Will I be allowed to see him?" asked Mary.

"I dare say. I dare say. We'll see about it," said the priest. "In the meantime, Mary, where will you be staying?"

"I don't know, Father. I thought you would tell me what to do. Is there anyone about that would take me in? I can pay my footing."

"Won't they be fighting for which of them will get you? There's Mrs. Dermody and her girls, and Mrs. Mulquin; and Tom Donohoe's wife, only they have a lot of children, God bless them, and few of the same about Killelagh! Tom has got share for two or three. But we'll lodge you among the neighbours, easy. Why, not one that ever knew you has forgot you, my poor child. The name of Mary O'Murrough is remembered by everybody. Stop a minute, and I'll be going along with you."

Father Fahy seized hat and stick, and he and Mary were soon threading the bog-paths and boreens[5] made to carry feet to the little gables and thatches that stand up against the mountain

---

5. Narrow country roads.

blue, or the green-and-purple and dun-brown of the low woods crowning the slopes and cushioning the hollows of Killelagh.

"Now, here's Mrs. Dermody! It's many a time she talks about your mother," said the priest cheerily.

The little farmhouse had a bare look, now that the elder-bushes were out of flower and out of leaf, and there were no dahlias making a column of colour at either side of the lintel. As the Father spoke, a head in a white frilled cap was thrust from the door, and Mrs. Dermody hastily put off the working apron and came forth to meet him.

"You're welcome, yer reverence," she said with a questioning glance at the stranger.

"Now, Mrs. Dermody, I've brought you an old friend, and one that we're glad to have back among us. Too many are going to America, and it's too few that come back. But here's one of the faithful ones."

"I'm glad to see her, Father. Is it Killarney or Ballyorglin, or furdher out In Kerry y' belong to?" said Mrs. Dermody, turning to the stranger."

"I belong to Killelagh," said Mary.

"Well, well," said Mrs. Dermody looking puzzled. I thought I remembered everybody that ever went out of Killelagh in my own time——"

She paused and gazed in the face of the new-comer inquiringly.

"My name is Mary O'Murrough."

"I only knew one of that name, but she was a beautiful girl, and very young. Nobody could ever forget her. She's comin' home to marry Shan Sullivan as soon as he gets out o' the trouble, God help him. Did y' see him lately, Father, and how soon can we get a sight of him?"

"Very soon, very soon," said the old man uneasily, "and Mary here is the first that has the right. Shan wrote for her to come home before he knew what was going to happen to him. Mary, you can see a bit of Shan's gable from here, just over towards Mangerton."

He pointed with his finger, directing Mary's eyes away from Mrs. Dermody's face that she might not see the look of consternation and incredulity that had settled on it; a look which Mary, spite of his kind endeavour, saw too well.

"I'm all that's left of the Mary O'Murrough you remember," she said with a poor little smile.

Mrs. Dermody gave a sharp cry and clapped her hands.

"Oh my poor girsha, it's thrue, it's thrue! For sure, now I look at y', I can see y' have a look of her in the eyes! Oh, God be good to y', for yer as big a ruin as yer old home over there, wid the roof off o' it!"

Mary's lip quivered; a storm long restrained broke loose in her, and she bent her head and wept tempestuously.

"Now, now, Mary!" cried the priest. "Mrs. Dermody, it's a shame for you. How can you expect a girl coming off her journey to look her best? And with bad news to meet her! She's just the same Mary O'Murrough that went out of this. None of us can be children always, as you ought to know, ma'am, that have reared your own daughters, and made women of them since Mary went away."

"It's thrue for y', Father," said Mrs. Dermody penitently. "A good many years has gone by, an' America's a hard place, whatever they say about it. Come in, Mary dear, an' rest yourself, an' have a cup o' tea."

CHAPTER ELEVEN
"WHAT'S LEFT OF HER."

Mrs. Dermody left the stranger resting on her own bed, and went out to meet her daughters, who had been attending to the animals in the yard, and driving home the hens from the field.

"You'd never guess who's in the house," she said. "Y' often heard tell of Mary O'Murrough. Well, she's home, an' Father Fahy has brought her to us for a lodgin'."

"It'll be hard on her, the way she'll find Shan," said Bess. "I thought she wasn't to come for another while."

"She's here, anyway. An' it'll be hard on Shan, too, to see her—what's left of her. If her own mother was to come back out o' the other world to meet her, she wouldn't know her. All the beauty is wore out of her, an' she's gone ould. That's yer America for y', that yer talkin' about goin' to."

"I don't want to go to America," said Bess, "not unless I go with Miles. I'm sorry for poor Mary O'Murrough, if that's the way with her."

Mrs. Dermody was too much shocked to take any notice of the mention of Miles. The tragedy of the parting of lovers had taken life and shape before her eyes, for the moment.

"Don't take any notice when you see her," she said. "Her long white face is not what anyone expected to see with her name to it, an' everybody praisin' the beauty of her when they mentioned her. You mustn't be lookin' at her strange, as if y' were missin' the round cheeks an' the rosy colour of her, an' the laughin' mouth an' the dimples. She's down enough, poor crature, without seein' the whole of her loss in other people's faces!"

Anne Bridget had been listening attentively, and the stranger's case appealed to her even more forcibly than it did to Bess. Happiness foregone had taken the light out of her own eyes early, and it moved her to hear that the much-lauded Mary O'Murrough had come home at last to her lover, and was beautiful no longer.

Mangerton was muffling his head in night clouds before the three Dermodys returned to the house, and found the stranger sitting alone at the fire.

"There now, I was tellin' them what a good rest y' were gettin'!" said Mrs. Dermody reproachfully.

"I couldn't rest," said Mary, looking wistfully at blooming Bess and fading Anne Bridget. "I'm sure the girls won't remember me. Kitty Casey didn't."

"Oh, I do remember you, a little," said Bess, eager to give comfort with words, but betraying her pity and dismay by her eyes.

"It's me that remembers you," said Anne Bridget, "an' I'd have knowed you out of a thousand. Bess wouldn't mind so well, because she's a good deal younger. Sure you're not so much changed, except that you're a bit thin, and tired-lookin'!"

"An' no wondher, with the throuble that's before y' on Shan," said Bess.

"Now, don't be talkin' about that," said Mrs. Dermody. "Sure it'll all be over afther a while. An' Mary'll be as happy as a cricket here wid ourselves, an' goin' to see him, an' watchin' for him to come out." So did the kind creatures strive to salve the wounds in a heart that the return wave of an ever outgoing ocean had washed over their threshold.

It was agreed that Mary could be lodged in the little loft over the kitchen, which was accordingly prepared for her; and Bess went down to the forge in the evening to see if there was "e'er a passin' cart would call at the inn at Ballyorglin" for her trunk. Miles was there to meet her, and Bess announced her news.

"Mary O'Murrough's come home, an' nobody would know her. Her good looks is all wrecked, an' she's nothin' but a shadda."

The men were silent and shocked at the girl's words and her tone of calamity.

"I was fearin' that," said Tom. "I knew Mary would come the minute she was bid. Pity it wasn't sooner. I'm sorry for her looks. A woman has beauty, an' so has a flower. It won't stan' time and roughness. Y'd betther take warnin' yerself, my girl, an' marry before it happens to y'."

"Aye, Bess!" said Miles, watching the changes in her usually bright face as the red light of the forge shone on it.

"What will Shan say? How will he bear it? He was always talkin' of the beauty of Mary, whinever he mentioned her. It'll break her to pieces if he doesn't be glad to see her."

"If he's a man, he won't mind," said Tom. "Look at my Meg. D'ye think she's the same young girl that she was whin I courted her? Why need I care if her beauty's gone? Was she as wise a woman, an' as good a wife, in the beginnin' as she is at the end?"

"Shan will care," said Miles. "A young man will care. It's a differ of a thing with you, father, that has your wife through all the changes."

"Oh," said Bess with sudden tears, "if we have to wait long enough, it's little y'll be wantin' me whin the time comes."

"Now y've done it, my boy!" said the blacksmith, lifting his hammer. "Take her away for a walk y' great bosthoon, an' make up for yer impudence!"

"Come on, Bess," said Miles. "Y' know well I didn't mean it. Y' know I'd want y' if yer two eyes was put out. I only want to say that I'd rather have y' as y' are."

When Mary lay down that night in her little loft on her bed of fresh straw that still smelt of the wheat, and her pillow stuffed with the down of the bog-blossoms, sleep did not come to her at once, tired as she was. Her senses were keenly alive to the presence of things long unknown to them, but familiar to memory. Resting in body and with closed eyes, she heard the murmur of subdued talk rising from the fireside of the kitchen below. A little light from the turf-blaze shone upward between the chinks of the slightly-boarded floor. The smell of the burning turf, the intonation even in murmur of the old sweet brogue, and many another small sound contributed to the assurance of home. In such a little loft she had slept as a child, with a sister who was taken out of it by angels, in a hungry year. So had she lain on the fresh straw and the bog-blossoms, listening to the murmurs of the talk of her elders from the fireside below. Were they really all gone, and had she ever been in America? Which was the dream, past or present, each looking so like the other as they hung round her, hand in hand, winged, and with loving faces? Father, mother, brothers and sisters, were with her now.

Shan had no part in this experience of the life of the child soul, wonderingly convinced of ancient things, undoubtingly satisfied with the security of visible surroundings and the infallible and beneficent power of mortal protectors. As the sounds from below ceased, and silence fell on the little household, the hours were still full of life for Mary, and rustling with intelligible whispers as they flitted past her.

After midnight a rising wind startled her with other suggestions, begot of moaning and threatening; and rain fell on her ears like the sound of her mother's weeping. Out of the storm came Shan's face, lighting up the world; and then the clouds again, and the separating sea, and the years among strangers, some of whom had grown to be friends, and were left behind, now and forever.

As the early hours of morning wore on, present circumstances reasserted themselves in all their realism and cruelty. The hurtling of the wind, the cry of the moor-fowl out of its sleep, were as echoes of painful thoughts. Once she got up and peered through the small window across the murky night landscape, in the direction of Shan's farm, which, in the darkness, was not to be seen. Later, as the sky cleared, she saw in the faint star-shine under the slanting eaves, her American trunk standing; in it, scrip for three hundred pounds—her earnings for Shan, the price of his future welfare, of her lost beauty, and of her youth outlived. Afterwards, all other thoughts were swept away in a great wave of grief that ran towards an unknown distance, through clouds and winds, and over fields and hills to the lover of her youth in his prison, suffering for some other man's wickedness, and dreaming of the young sweetheart he was never again to set eyes upon.

When grief had so risen to its climax sleep took pity. Anne Bridget creeping up the little ladder to the loft, found Mary in a sound slumber, and went creeping down again.

"I wouldn't say but it's in her first sleep she is," was her remark; and mother and daughters moved about quietly, fearing to recall "the crature, God help her!" too soon to her sorrow.

She had scarcely eaten her breakfast, when Father Fahy appeared to tell Mary that he was on his way to see Shan, to inform him of her arrival, and endeavour to make arrangements for a visit from her to the prison at the first available opportunity.

"Mayn't I go with you now, Father?" pleaded Mary.

"No, child, you're too tired, and besides, Shan isn't expecting to see you. We must prepare him for a surprise."

"Surprise enough!" muttered Mrs. Mulquin, who had come early to see the returned exile, and whose bitter thoughts about America were not sweetened by the sight of the ravages made by time and rough toil in the person of Mary O'Murrough.

Mrs. Dermody frowned at her, at the same moment shouting at an intrusive hen, in order to drown her neighbour's thoughtless murmuring.

Mary was obedient, and when the priest went his way, she sat down at the fireside, picking up a half-knitted stocking which Mrs. Dermody had laid down, and making the needles fly between her fingers.

"Can't y' be at peace, an' rest yerself?" protested her hostess, looking on with admiration.

"You'll have to give me work," said Mary. "I'm used to it, and I couldn't live without it."

"Oh, then, we can give y' plenty," said Anne Bridget. "I wish I could knit as fast as you do." Many friends dropped in that evening to see if it was true that Mary O'Murrough had come home to Killelagh. That, after all the years, she should have returned to find Shan in prison was recognised as a painful fatality, a tragic chapter in a story of patience and constancy. The change in her appearance and her health gave an added touch of pathos to the situation, and, spite of good-natured efforts to conceal it, the general impression of dismay was visible in every countenance.

Mary saw it all with a pale smile, grateful for, but uncomforted by the warmth of the welcoming that was poured out on her. Tom

Donohoe the blacksmith and his gentle motherly wife sat one on each side of her, and talked to her about Shan.

"There isn't such a man in the county of Kerry," said Tom; "clever at his business, an' keepin' a hould on everything, an' a good son, with the blessin' of his dyin' mother; humourin' that quare ould father o' his, an' never as much as lookin' the way a girl went, because she wasn't Mary, an' her in America! D'ye mind, Meg, the way he used to talk to you on' me about his Mary O'Murrough?"

"Sure I do that!" said Meg. "'I love the ground she walks on, Mrs. Donohoe,' he says to me, 'though it's American ground, to my sorra!'"

"'Wait a bit, Shan,' says I. 'It won't be always American ground.'"

"'It's true for you, Mrs. Donohoe,' says he, 'for she'll be coming with the spring flowers,' says he, 'an' ne'er a one o' them same to compare with her,' says Shan, says he."

A little faint rose grew on Mary's cheek listening, and she gathered up these and other sweet words repeated to her, and hid them in her heart with fear and gladness.

CHAPTER TWELVE
"WHY WOULDN'T IT BE A COMFORT TO HIM TO SEE HER?"

In a gleam of wintry sunshine Mary walked across the fields and through the gaps, to the ruin of the cottage where she had been born.

Scarcely a bit of the old roof remained only wrecked walls, broken window sockets and an entrance without a door. Nettles were growing beside the hearthstone, the black stain behind it showing where the home fire had warmed father, mother, and children; a little crowd, with laughter and prattle, song and prayer, gathered round it.

She sat on a fallen fragment of the wall and closed her eyes, and lived in the old scenes, seeing the faces and hearing the voices.

Surely the loving spirits would come round her now, here; years of heaven would not make them forget her. Time was nothing where they were, nor place, nor were there any conditions of limitation. Of all that she had been well instructed and long assured. If they could have forgotten her, had not her prayers to God in their name forged links to bind their memory? In whatever language Mary might have formulated these thoughts, if called on to utter them, such convictions, expressed or unexpressed, were as absolute to her as her own identity.

A footstep roused her, and Father Fahy appeared in the broken doorway.

"Now Mary O'Murrough, my poor child, what are you doing here, God help you?"

"I couldn't but come to see my own, your reverence."

"Now, now, now! Isn't heaven all round you; and why can't you see them any minute, everywhere, without coming to break your heart, and their hearts too, going back on troubles that they're laughing at long ago?"

"You never taught us to think they could break their hearts in heaven, Father!"

"Now, don't catch me up, Mary! You know what I mean. They wouldn't like to see you fretting."

"When am I to go to see Shan, Father?"

"Come out of this, child, and I'll walk across the fields with you."

Mary obeyed.

"When are you going to see him, Father?"

"I have been to see him, Mary. He's brave and well."

"When am I to go?"

"You're in a great hurry, child. Why are you in such a hurry?"

"I am in a hurry. I want to see Shan."

"Of course, of course. And you will see him—after a while."

"Does he not want to see me?" said Mary, with a sudden chill of the heart.

"Well now, Mary, he does want to see you. But he's proud, the poor fellow, and he can't bear to think of you seeing him in the prison."

"Oh, Father! He couldn't mean it! Am I to wait all that time? After comin' from America, an' him never to set eyes on me? What do I care about the prison when I want to see Shan?"

"You're a brave girl, and I told him so. And he said I needn't tell him that the sun was warm, and the grass was green; and a few more things like that. One small bit of praise he gave you was—only that you were an angel. But we must allow that Shan's a little bit proud and stubborn when he takes a notion. And he's full sure that it would only make him ten times more miserable if you were to see him first, after all the years, in the dress and in the position of a convict."

Mary was silent under this fresh blow. Her lips were paler than ever when she said at last: "It's hard, Father."

"It is hard, Mary. I don't deny it. But we've got a man to deal with who has a good share of trouble on his back, and we must humour him. You can write to him, and I'll take your messages. You have come through plenty that has taught you patience, and you've only got to be patient a little longer."

"What does he want me to do?" asked Mary, after another silent appeal to her courage.

"He wants you to amuse yourself and be happy, so he does, poor Shan."

"Amuse myself, an' him in prison? Is it a foolish young girl he thinks me still, Father?"

"You never were that, Mary. But he wants you to make the best of it. An' when he meets you, it'll be in his own clothes and walkin' in the fields of Killelagh. That's about what he means in it, and if I know you at all you're not the girl to contrary him."

"What am I to do with myself here in the meantime?"

"Well now, one thing you could do, if you're the angel Shan takes you for. There's poor old Owny, Shan's father, a miserable sick and sorry old man, and one that is to blame for the long separation of the pair of you. He's gone near blind and near dead with grief about Shan's misfortune, and still God's not taking him yet, and he's lonely, and every way unhappy. If you would set your mind to it and look after him a little, it would be as great a charity as ever a woman put her hand to."

"I'll do anything I can for him," said Mary.

"God bless you, and do. I'll go up and speak to him, and tell him you're coming to see him."

Long accustomed to patience, Mary made no further complaint. If a meeting in prison, their first meeting after so many years, would fill his cup of bitterness to overflowing, then she must not think of seeing Shan. She must wait at least for some change in his mood, and meanwhile let her faithful letters and her messages through the priest assure him of her nearness and her sympathy.

Old Owny was sitting in his straw chair at the fire when Mary came in to him.

"Is it you, Mary? Father Fahy said you would come, but I thought you wouldn't. We kep' you away too long, waitin' for the best, an' now all's at the worst. Come a bit neardher to me, for I'm that blind I can only see a sketch of you that might be anybody at all, an' the shape of some kind of a face is all that's plain to me."

"I'm glad to see you—I'm glad to be home again," said Mary. "God's good, an' things'll be better by and by."

"Oh, that's Mary that said it," said the old man delightedly. "Sure I'd know your voice anywhere, acushla. Not a bit changed it is. 'Mary's voice is the blackbird in the spring morning before the light's in the sky,' Shan used to say to me. An' so it is still, Mary, an' it's good o' you to be comin' to see the like o' me, a poor miserable ould creature that's not long for this world; an' sorry I am to be lavin' it with things not the way I would like them to be."

"You're not leavin' it yet," said Mary. "Shan will soon be coming back to you, and then we'll all be happy."

"The pair o' y'll be happy, I hope and pray. But I'll not live to see it, I'm feared! 'Deed an' y' will,' says Father Fahy, says he to me, 'an' if you don't see it sittin' there in your ould straw chair,' says he, 'sure y'll get a betther view from where y'll be. For you're sorry for any sins y' iver done, Owny,' says he, 'an' you're bearin' yer sickness well,' says he, 'an' the Lord wants no more than that, for He done the rest Himself long ago,' says his reverence, says he."

"I'm glad you're that comforted," said Mary in her sweet mellow tones, answering, tearfully and heartfully, to Shan's lover-like words about them. "It's Father Fahy who knows how to put hope and heart into a body. An' 'twas him that sent me here to talk to y', an' nurse y' up a bit."

"Aye, aye, Mary, an' 'twas you was the good nurse to your own mother; and God bless you, an' thry to hould me together till Shan comes back, for, if it was plazin' to His Majesty, I wouldn't like to die without settin' my two eyes on my little boy's face wanst more. Not that I can see a dale of features in anyone now, but I'd know it was himself whin he'd say, 'Father, won't y' give us yer blessin'?'"

After this welcome Mary made the nursing of Owny her daily occupation, such tender charity to the lonely old man filling a great vacancy, and hastening the slow-footed hours. Every day she took the uphill path to the little farm, which was already showing dolorous signs of its master's absence, and returned in the evening to sleep at Mrs. Dermody's. Growing bolder, she seized the opportunity when Owny slumbered from weakness, to walk about the yards and fields, observing the things that were going wrong, and striving to discover whether she herself might or might not make an effort towards putting them right. At favourable moments she gathered from Owny information as to the requirements of the season for land and beasts, and quietly took the direction of such matters into her hands. The animals were properly housed and fed as Shan would have had them, the fences were mended, the turf was cut and put to dry, the manure for the potatoes was gathered and stored. People passing by the Sullivans' holding remarked that Owny was "managin' wonderful" without his son, considering his age and illness, and that it was well for him to have Mary O' Murrough to carry out his orders.

In the late hours of the evening she was helpful with knitting or sewing, her superior cleverness and experience giving her a power admired and appreciated by the Dermodys. At the same time, her singing of the old songs treasured in her memory during the years of absence was an attraction to the neighbours, and many a one came dropping in for an hour before bedtime to hear Mary O'Murrough lilting the "Poor Croppy Boy" and the "Boys o' Wexford."[6] Owny's praise of her voice, and Shan's words of delight in it, let fall by the old man, had given her courage to exercise this gift left to her still, though her beauty might be gone. If Owny's failure of sight had deprived him of the ability to criticise her looks, the keenness of his other faculties had enabled him to bestow on her this courage and comfort. As the people grew accustomed to her altered appearance, and became acquainted with her in her new character, the painful consciousness of change in herself was less acute, and the cheerful spirit of hope which was natural to her was steadily striving to reassert itself.

She ceased to fear absolutely that the lover's messages which came from Shan were received by one who was in reality a stranger to him. Faint expectation of a return of joy was stirring in her heart when the young year stepped over the shamrocks and daisies from March into April, with feet still rosy from cold, and wet with dew, but gleaming in golden sandals of intermittent sunshine.

One evening, when spring seemed to stand a-tiptoe on the blue-grey hills watching across the world for the coming of summer, with wings half spread ready to fly to meet her, Mary came slowly through the fields after her day's attendance on Owny. Nearing

---

6. Songs relating to the 1798 rebellion in Ireland. Croppy was a name for a rebel in a reference to the short hair preferred by supporters of the French Revolution. Wexford was one of the centres of the rebellion.

the gap in the fence which would lead her by a "short cut", she came on Bess and Miles sitting together on the other side with their backs towards her, their heads just above the level of the "ditch". Thinking to speak to them as she passed through the gap, she was arrested by a few words from Miles in the suddenly raised voice of one who is uttering an opinion maintained against all contradiction.

"Of course, it is only to save herself from more sorra that Shan is keepin' her away. Why wouldn't it be a comfort to him to see her?"

Mary stood still, gazing with eyes that did not see, and ears that heard no more. After a minute's interval she turned on her steps, and went across the fields by another footpath.

A storm of passion was in her heart, remorse for her own stupid obedience, disgust at her cowardly patience, anger even at Father Fahy's mild, misunderstanding counsels. Would the night ever pass, and the morning come, so that she might start at once to bring comfort to Shan in his prison? O wicked meekness! O mistaken submission to a sentence which she had accepted as cruel only to herself, but which in reality was punishment of another already so undeservedly afflicted.

The barriers erected by her patience against the eagerness of her desire had been swept away by a word, and next morning at cockcrow would have seen Mary on her way to the County Gaol, had she not remembered that on one certain day of the month only could Shan be visited. The day was near, but a further pause in her present state of mind appeared unendurable.

On the evening before the longed-for morning, she went to look for Father Fahy, and found him walking up and down the road before his cottage, reading his breviary.

"Tomorrow's the day for visiting Shan, Father. I've made up my mind to go to see him."

"No, no, child. Don't go back of your word. Didn't you promise me you wouldn't?"

"I see now that he wanted to save me the trouble and the pain. It couldn't be that he wouldn't find comfort in seeing me. I'll make him feel that it was far more pain to me to have to stay away, and that it's glad I am to see him, if he was in a worse place than a prison."

The old priest looked at her, and saw that some change had taken place in her. Here was passion instead of patience, energy for action instead of passive fortitude. No use he thought, in striving with her further. "May I go with you, Mary?"

"No, thank you, Father. I'll go by myself. I want you to tell me the way to go, and the hours, and the rules, and all about it."

The Father shut his book and took her into his house, and wrote on a piece of paper all the directions needed for her journey and her visit.

"I'm going to see Shan tomorrow," she said to the Dermodys next morning early. "Father Fahy knows."

"God bless y', an' I'm glad," said Mrs. Dermody. "It's too hard they were on y' when they were keepin' y' back."

"She's wonderful cool over it," said Bess to Anne Bridget after she had gone. "If it was me gain' to see Miles after all them years, I think I would be in bigger excitement."

"Few words says most," said Anne Bridget, going on with her knitting. "I wish to God she was back, out of it."

The white heat of Mary's passion carried her swiftly over the miles she had to walk, and a short railway journey brought her to her destination.

7

Selected Poems

From *Vagrant Verses*
London: Elkin Mathews, [1899].

THE BUILDERS
I saw the builders laying
Stones on the grassy sod,
And people praised them, saying:
"A fane to the mighty God
Shall rise aloft in glory,
Pillars and arches wide,
Windows stained with the story
Of Christ the Crucified."

I saw the broken boulders
Lie in the waving grass,
Flung down from bending shoulders,
And said, "Our lives must pass
Ere wide cathedral spreading
Can span this mossy field
Where kine are slowly treading
And flowers their honey yield.

"Oh, dreaming builders, tarry!
Unchain your souls from toil,
Leave the rock in the quarry,
The bloom upon the soil;

For life is short, my brothers, —
And labour wastes it sore, —
Why toil to gladden others
When you shall breathe no more?

"Oh! come with footstep springing,
With empty hands and free,
And tread the green earth singing
'The world was made for me!'
Pray amid nature's sweetness
In pillared forest glade,
Content with the incompleteness
Of fanes that the Lord has made!"

The builders, never heeding,
Kept piling stone on stone,
Their hands with toil were bleeding—
I went my way alone.
Prayed in the forest temple
And ate the wild-bee's store;
My life was pure and simple—
What would the Lord have more.

The years, like one long morning,
They all flew swiftly by;
Old age with little warning
Came creeping softly nigh.
Now (be we all forgiven!) I longed to see, alas!
What the builders had raised to heaven
Instead of the tender grass.

I heard a sweet bell ringing
Over the world so wide;
I heard a sound of singing

Across the eventide.
What sight my soul bewilders
Beneath the sunset's glow?
The fane that the dreaming builders
Were building long ago!

'Tis not the sculptured portal,
Or windows jewelled wide,
With joys of the life immortal,
And woes of Him who died,
That fill my soul with wonder,
And drain my heart of tears,
And ask with voice of thunder,
"Where are thy wasted years!"

But a thousand thousand creatures
Kneel down where grew the sod,
And hear with glowing features
The words that breathe of God.
Alone and empty-handed,
I wait by the open door:
Such work hath the Lord commanded,
And I can work—no more!

The builders, never heeding,
They lie and take their rest,
And hands no longer bleeding
Are folded on each breast—
The grass waves o'er them sleeping,
And flowerets red and white,
Where I kneel above them weeping,
And whisper, "You were right."

A STOLEN VISIT

When you are wrapped in happy sleep,
I walk about your house by night,
With many a wistful, stealthy peep
At what I've loved by morning light.

Your head is on the pillow laid,
My feet are where your footsteps were;
Your soul to other lands has strayed,
My heart can hear you breathe and stir.

I seat me in your wonted chair,
And ope your book a little space;
I touch the flowers that knew your care,
The mirror that reflects your face.

I kiss the pen that spoke your thought,
The spot whereon you knelt to pray,
The message with your wisdom fraught
Writ down on paper yesterday,

The garment that you lately wore,
The threshold that your step goes by,
The music that you fingered o'er,
The picture that contents your eye.

Yet when you wake from happy sleep,
And, busy here, and busy there,
You take your wonted morning peep
At what is good and what is fair,

"She has been here," you will not say,
My prying face you will not find;
You'll think, "She is a mile away,"
My love hath left no mark behind.

SNOW AND FAMINE

What are you weaving, silent Snow?
To and fro, sad and slow,
While the winds are keening low,
Weird and low, thick with woe;
Hoarse and sudden, sobbing loud,
Shrill with woe. Ah! I know,
Well I know, you weave a shroud,
Mournful Snow!

What are you hiding, eerie Snow?
Pallid so, crouching low,
With your trailing garment's flow,
Spread beneath the moon's pale glow.
What do you hide, so cold and dread,
Down below? Ah! I know,
You swathe the lone unburied dead,
Ghastly Snow!

Where do you drift, mysterious Snow?
To and fro, sad and slow,
While the rough winds gasp with woe,
Through the cabin door you go,
Treading over the hearth and floor,
Lying low. Yes, I know,
The home-blaze leaps there never more,
Chilly Snow!

Is it Christmas, wandering Snow?
To and fro, roaming so;
We in the mountains cannot know,
Sunk in woe, dying slow.
Is the Saviour born on earth?
Ah! 'tis so; yes, I know,
We'll warm us at His heavenly hearth,
Kindly Snow!

From *Spirit and Dust. Poems* London: Elkin Mathews, 1908.

MARY IN BETHLEHEM

Sleep, my babe, upon my breast,
Sleep thou now, and take thy rest;
Ass and ox are kindly near,
Loving eyes do watch thee, dear.
Stars are high o'er Bethlehem,
Baby-eyes cannot see them;
Thou didst make them, every one,
And all that they look down upon.

Wondrous Lord who built the light,
Hiding here in wintry night!
What a secret, my sweet son,
Mother's heart must bear alone—
Babe of mine, and yet the great
God of Abraham, incarnate;
Sleep thou yet, and take thy rest,
Soon thou'lt wake and quit the nest.

Tender body, tender eyes,
Babe so simple, great All-wise,
Thou art only babe to me—
Sleep, the years will come for thee.
Men are cruel, baby dear,
Strong in hate and base in fear;
Hold them in thy hand and sleep,
Let thy mother wake and weep.

By the way a sharp thorn grows,
Thou shalt wear it on thy brows;
On the earth there stands a tree,

Nigh full grown, that waits for thee.
It will blossom every spring,
Rare and sweet its blossoming;
It hath struck a deathless root,
It shall bear a wondrous fruit.

Years will come and lead thee forth;
All thy future heaven is worth;
In my heart a sword is worn,
Sword that turned when thou wert born.
All the way I'll walk with thee
Through the thorns and to the tree;
Sleep, my babe upon my breast,
While thou mayst, and take thy rest.

Son and God, who cling'st to me;
Shall my feet yet follow thee
Far beyond the thorns and rood,
Far beyond the scourge and blood,
Up the path of light that runs
To thy home beyond the suns?
Sleep, my babe, upon my breast,
Sleep thou now and take thy rest!

OURS
Little gay chamber, thickset walls of gold,
Windows full of the beauty of the green
Shelter of trees, heaven's mystical palisade;
Limning of faded saints that lurk between
The brightnesses, like stories long since told;
Soft darkling curtains bringing fitful shade.

Here lived in holy joy, and loved, and died
We who are separate now, yet still are one.

Here wakened we to hear the blackbird sing
His matins, and beheld new-open-eyed
The dawn make signal when the night was done;
Here morns slid by like opals down a string.

Here laughed, together glad, and here died we;
For what is now of me is not what was
Of both, and is of both in the sweet elsewhere,
My hand in thine, e'en though I may not see
Thine eyes as thou see'st mine in the long pause
That holds my feet till I may run to thee.

From *Dreams and Realities* London; Edinburgh, Sands & Co., 1916.

DREAD
The world's afire and none to save
Wind howl and rain rave,
The world is all a wandering grave!

The earth is but a blackened stone
Whirling round a greater one, —
Frozen sun whose light is done!

Shepherd, what use in your crook?
Scientist, for your outlook?
Poet, who's to read your book?

All the jewels of the east,
Gold and silver of the west,
Buried are in ruin's breast.

Wheel of terror, dreadful ball
Black with death, containing all
Bodies built since Adam's fall!

Now are all the souls were born
To your years of night and morn
Gathered by an angel's horn.

THE FACTORY GIRL

Chose it instead of America, ye see it was neardher home.
"Plenty of work in the North," they said, an' so I riz an' come.
Nine of us on the bit o' land, an' failded at last wid the rint;
No price to be got for the cow at all, an' the lan'lord as hard as flint!

Rest o' thim wint to the Huts. I thought I'd be able to arn
Somethin' to help thim along, workin' up here at the yarn.
But what wid the sickness an' fines, an' the wages so tar'ble small
I'd niver a ha'penny to sind—I wuz no help to them at all.

Fines on all that I wove. My loom was bad an' it run
Wrong wid the web; an' the weavin', 'twas ruined afore it was done.
Fines for a mouthful of water whin yer heart was just ready to burst
Wid the roastin' heat o' the place, an' the ragin' fire o' yer thirst.

Off'ner sick nor well, even at the best o' your prime;
For, ye see, yer drippin' wet at yer work the whole o' the time.
Only a shift an' a petticoat on ye, not enough o' clo'es
To cover a dacent girl, an' keep her modest, God knows!

An' thin, whin the bell is rung, an' ye run out into the street
It's the sharp east wind or the frost that yer bones have got to meet.
An' yer bit of a shawl is not much use to keep out the stabs o' the could;
It's that way whin yer young, but ye never live to be ould.

A quare place to be sick in. Aye, deed, so ye may say!
Four of us lies in the bed at night, I have it myself all day.
Will ye write to my mother an' tell her my heart is sore
That I hadn't a penny to send her — my love, an' nothin' more.

For whin I'd arned a shillin' an' threepence, the threepence was
    all I'd to get;
The shillin' wint for the fine on the crucked loom that'd set
Iverything wrong as it wint. What mather, 'twas me had to pay—
I'd betther starved where I wuz in the fields 'twixt the bog an' the
    say.

Slime an' dirt where ye stand at yer work, an' the smells'd dhrive
    ye mad;
Yer tould to go to hell if ye cry, but hell can't be half as bad.
I know I'm goin' somewhere, docthor, I see it like prent in your
    face;
But I hope it won't be *there*. Thank God there's another place!

Select Bibliography

Works by Rosa Mulholland (Lady Gilbert, Ruth Murray)

Novels

'Ruth Murray'. *Dunmara*. 3 vols. (London, Smith, Elder, 1864). Republished as *The Story of Ellen* (London, Burns & Oates; New York, Benziger Brothers, 1907).
Charles Dickens, Wilkie Collins. *No Thoroughfare; to which is added The Late Miss Hollingford*. (Leipzig, Tauchnitz, 1868).
Hester's History. A Novel (London, n.p., 1869).
The Wicked Woods of Tobereevil (London, Chapman and Hall, 1872).
The Wild Birds of Killeevy (London, Burns and Oates, [1883]).
Hetty Gray, or, Nobody's Bairn (London, Blackie, 1884).
Marcella Grace (London, Kegan, Paul & Trench. 1886; James H. Murphy (ed.), Washington, DC, Maunsel, 2001).
The Late Miss Hollingford (London, Blackie & Son, 1886).
A Fair Emigrant. A Novel (London; Edinburgh, Kegan, Paul & Trench, 1888).
Gianetta, a Girl's Story of Herself (London, Blackie & Son, 1889).
The Mystery of Hall-in-the-Wood (London, Sunday School Union, 1893).
Banshee Castle (London, Blackie & Son, 1895). Republished as *The Girls of Banshee Castle* (London, Blackie & Son, [1925]).
Nanno. A Daughter of the State (London, Grant Richards, 1899).
Onora (London, Grant Richards, 1900).
Terry, or, She Ought to Have Been a Boy (London, Blackie & Son, [1900]).
Cynthia's Bonnet Shop (London, Blackie & Son, 1901).
The Tragedy of Chris (London; Edinburgh, Sands & Co. 1903).
The Squire's Granddaughters (London, Burns & Oates; New York, Benzigers Brothers, 1903).
A Girl's Ideal (London, Blackie & Son, 1905).
Our Sister Maisie (London, Blackie & Son, 1907).
The Return of Mary O'Murrough (London; Edinburgh, Sands & Co., 1908).
Cousin Sara. A Story of Arts and Crafts (London, Blackie & Son, 1909).
Father Tim (London; Edinburgh, Sands & Co., 1910).
Agatha's Hard Saying (New York, Benziger, 1911).
The O'Shaughnessy Girls (London, Blackie & Son, 1911).
Fair Noreen (London, Blackie & Son, 1912).
Twin Sisters. An Irish Tale (London, Blackie & Son, 1913).
The Cranberry Claimants (London, Sands & Co. 1913).

Our School Friends. A Tale of Modern Life. (London, Blackie & Son, 1914).
Norah of Waterford (London; Edinburgh, Sands & Co., 1915).
The Daughter in Possession. The Story of a Great Temptation (London, Blackie & Son, 1915).
Narcissa's Ring (London, Blackie & Son, 1916).
O'Loghlin of Clare (London, Edinburgh, Sands & Co., 1916).

Children's Works
The Little Flower Seekers, being adventures of Trot and Daisy in a Wonderful Garden by Moonlight (London; Belfast, [1873]).
Five Little Farmers (London; Belfast, Marcus Ward & Co., 1876).
Puck and Blossom, a Fairy Tale (London; Belfast, Marcus Ward & Co., [1879]).
Four Little Mischiefs (London, Blackie & Son, 1883).

Collections of Short Stories and Selected Individual Short Stories
'Irené'. *Cornhill Magazine* 5:28 (1862), pp. 478–80.
'My First Picture'. *London Society* 1:4 (1862), pp. 289–302.
'Bet's Match-Making'. *All the Year Round*, 15:356 (1866), pp. 134–8.
'The Ghost of Rath'. *All the Year Round.* 15:364 (1866), pp. 329–66.
Eldergowan; or twelve months of my life; and other tales (London; Belfast, Marcus Ward, 1874).
'The Hungry Death'. *All the Year Round* (1880), pp. 61–72.
'The Girl from under the Lake. A Fairy Tale.' *Irish Monthly* (1881). 9:98, pp. 395–404; 9:99, pp. 453–64; 9:100, pp. 536–45; 9:101, pp. 569–77; 9:103, pp. 627–35.
The Walking Trees, and Other Tales (Dublin, Gill & Son, 1885).
The Haunted Organist of Hurly Burly, and Other Stories. (n.p., n.d., [1891]).
Marigold, and Other Stories (Dublin, Eason & Son, 1894).
Our Own Story, and Other Tales (London, Catholic Truth Society, [1896]).

Poetry Collections
Vagrant Verses (London, Elkin Mathews, [1899]).
Spirit and Dust. Poems (London, Elkin Mathews, 1908).
Dreams and Realities (London, Edinburgh, Sands & Co., 1916).

Drama
Pat. A Miniature Farce. Irish Monthly. 8:90 (1880), pp. 629–40.
'The Duchess Pepita, A Miniature Extravaganza'. *Irish Monthly*, 9:91 (1881), pp. 1–8; 9:92 (1881), pp. 62–70.
The Irish Heiress, a Miniature Comedy in Two Acts. Irish Monthly. 9:95 (1881), 236–44; 9:96 (1881), 289–97.
Our Boycotting, a Miniature Comedy (Dublin, M.H. Gill & Son, 1907). [Reproduced in Heidi Hansson and James H. Murphy (eds.), *Fictions of the Irish Land War* (Oxford, Peter Lang, 2014), pp. 191–212].

Selected Essays, Biographies and Edited Work

'Jottings in Lancashire,' *Irish Monthly*, 10:103 (1882), pp. 38–45; 10:104 (1882) pp. 97–105; 10:105 (1882) pp. 132–40.

'Fra Bartolommeo, the Great Dominican Painter'. *Irish Monthly*, 10:108 (1882) pp. 391–400; 10:109 (1882), pp. 473–81.

Gems for the Young from Favourite Poets (Dublin, Gill and Son, 1884). [editor]

'Saint Restituta. Virgin-Martyr,' *Irish Monthly* 15:173 (1887), pp. 603–5.

'Dublin Castle.' *Woman's World*. 1:7 (1888), pp. 304–9.

Calendar of Ancient Records of Dublin in the possession of the Municipal Corporation of that city. [Vol. I.-VII. edited by John T. Gilbert. Vol. VIII. edited by Lady Gilbert.] (Dublin, Joseph Dollard, 1889).

'Mary Redmond, the Young Irish Sculptor'. *Irish Monthly* 17:194 (1889), pp. 416–22.

'Irish Painters in this Present Year,' *Irish Monthly* 17:195 (1889), pp. 481–6.

'Our Poets. No 23. William Butler Years.' *Irish Monthly*. 17:194 (1889), pp. 365–71.

'A Holy Pilgrimage', *Irish Monthly* 17:197, (1889), pp. 582–5.

'Linen-Weaving in Skibbereen.' *Irish Monthly*, 18:201 (1890), pp. 145–8.

'The Irish Cistercians of Mount Mellary,' *Irish Monthly* 18:202 (1890), pp. 210–14.

Father Mathew, a Biography (Dublin, Eason & Son; London, S. Bagster & Son, [1891]). [With John Francis Maguire.]

'Wanted an Irish Novelist', *Irish Monthly*. 19:217 (1891), pp. 368–73.

'At Killarney.' *Irish Monthly*. 19.220 (1891), 505–10; 'At Cork.' *Irish Monthly*, 19:221 (1891), pp. 561–7; 'At Youghal.' *Irish Monthly*, 19:222 (1891), pp. 617–28; 'At Howth.' *Irish Monthly*, 20:223 (1892), pp. 33–7.

'About Roses. A Dublin Letter to an Australian Cousin', *Irish Monthly*, 20:228 (1892), pp. 281–6.

'About Ghosts. A Letter to an Australian Cousin', *Irish Monthly*, 20:229 (1892), pp. 337–41.

'About Bogs. A Letter to an Australian Cousin', *Irish Monthly*, 20:232 (1892), pp. 505–8.

Atkinson, Sarah. *Essays* (Dublin, M.H. Gill and Son, 1895). [With a memoir by Rosa Mulholland.]

'Our Lady's Hospice for the Dying.' *Irish Monthly*, 23:269 (1895), pp. 585–9.

'Today and Yesterday in the Children's Hospital.' *Irish Monthly*, 25:287 (1897), pp. 250–55.

'The Prayer of Mary, Queen,' *Irish Monthly*, 26:299 (1898), pp. 225–7.

'Before the Tabernacle', *Irish Monthly*, 30:350 (1902), pp. 453–4.

Life of Sir John T. Gilbert, LL.D., F.S.A., Irish Historian and Archivist, Vice-President of the Royal Irish Academy, Secretary of the Public Records Office of Ireland (London. Longmans and Co., 1905).

Prince and Saviour, the Story of Jesus Simply Told for the Young (Dublin, Gill and Son, 1907).

'Mrs Meynell's Poems.' *Irish Monthly* 41:482 (1913), pp. 427–32.

'The Late Father Matthew Russell, S.J. An Anniversary Sketch.' *Irish Monthly* 41:483 (1913), pp. 465–75.

'The Memoirs of Father Matthew Russell, SJ.' *Irish Monthly* (1921), 49:573, pp. 89–96; 49:574, pp. 133–40; 49:575, pp. 177–83; 49:576, pp. 221–7; 49:577, pp. 265–9.

Further Reading

Binckes, Faith, and Kathryn Laing. *Hannah Lynch (1859–1904): Irish Writer, Cosmopolitan, New Woman* (Cork. Cork University Press, 2019).

Cahill, Susan. 'Making Spaces for the Irish Girl: Rosa Mulholland and Irish Girls in Fiction at the turn of the Century.' In Kristine Moruzi and Michelle J. Smith (eds.) *Colonial Girlhood in Literature, Culture and History, 1840–1950* (London, Palgrave Macmillan, 2014), pp. 167–79.

Collins, Lucy (ed.), *Poetry by Women in Ireland: A Critical Anthology (1870–1970)* (Liverpool, Liverpool University Press, 2012).

Corporaal, Marguérite. *Relocated Memories: The Great Famine in Irish and Diaspora Fiction, 1846–1870* (Syracuse, NY, Syracuse University Press, 2017).

———, C.T. Cusack and Lindsay Janssen (eds), *Recollecting Hunger: An Anthology. Cultural Memories of the Great Famine in Irish and British Fiction, 1847–1920* (Dublin, Irish Academic Press, 2012).

Cusack, C.T. 'Sunk in the Mainstream. Irish Women Writers, Canonicity, and Famine Memory, 1892–1910.' In Kathryn Laing and Sinéad Mooney (eds.), *Irish Women's Writing at the Turn of the Twentieth Century. Alternative Histories, New Narratives* (Brighton, Edward Everett Root, 2020), pp. 37–48.

Dalby, Richard. 'Rosa Mulholland, Mistress of the Macabre.' *The Green Book: Writings on Irish Gothic, Supernatural and Fantastic Literature*, 9 (2017), pp. 19–23.

Dalby, Richard (ed.). *Not to Be Taken at Bed-Time and Other Strange Stories by Rosa Mulholland* (Dublin, Swan River Press, 2019).

Hansson, Heidi, 'From Reformer to Sufferer: The Returning Exile in Rosa Mulholland's Fiction.' In Michael Böss, Irene Gilsenan Nordin and Britta Oinder (eds.), *Re-Mapping Exile: Realities and Metaphors in Irish Literature and History* (Aarhus, Aarhus University Press, 2006), pp. 89–106.

Hansson, Heidi, and James H. Murphy (eds.), *Fictions of the Irish land War* (Oxford, Peter Lang, 2014).

IMO. *Priests and People: A No Rent Romance*. 3 vols. By the Author of '*Lotus*' and '*A New Marguerite.*' (London, Eden, Remington, 1891). [Reprinted 1979 by Garland].

Laird, Heather. 'Decentring the Irish land War: Women, Politics and the Private Sphere.' In Fergus Campbell and Tony Varley (eds), *Land Questions in Modern Ireland* (Manchester, Manchester University Press, 2013), pp. 175–93.

Moruzi, Kristine. *Constructing Girlhood through the Periodical Press, 1850–1915* (Aldershot, Ashgate, 2012).

Murphy, James H. *Catholic Fiction and Social Reality in Ireland, 1873–1922* (Westport CT, Greenwood, 1997), pp. 16–17, 31–5, 54–6, 69–71.

———. '"Insouciant Rivals of Mrs Barton": Gender and Victorian Aspiration in George Moore and the Women Novelists of *The Irish Monthly*', in Margaret Kelleher and James H. Murphy (eds.), *Gender Perspectives on Nineteenth-Century Ireland: Public and Private Spheres* (Dublin, Irish Academic Press, 1997), pp. 221–8.

———. '"Things Which Seem to You Unfeminine": Gender and Nationalism in the Fiction of some Upper Middle Class Catholic Women Novelists, 1880–1910.' In Kathryn Kirkpatrick (ed.), *Border Crossings: Irish Women Writers and National Identities.* (Tuscaloosa, University of Alabama Press, 2000), pp. 58–78.

———. 'Catholics and Fiction during the Union, 1801–1922.' In John Wilson Foster (ed.) *The Cambridge Companion to the Irish Novel* (Cambridge, Cambridge University Press, 2006), pp 97–112.

———. *Irish Novelists and the Victorian Age* (Oxford, Oxford University Press, 2011), pp. 175–8, 181–4, 245–9, 260.

———. 'The Dark Arts of the Critic: Yeats and William Carleton.' In Marjorie Howes and Joseph Valente (eds), *Yeats and Afterwords* (Notre Dame, Notre Dame University Press, 2014), pp 80–99.

———. '"She's nothin' but a shadda": The Politics of Marriage in Late Mulholland.' In Anna Pilz and Whitney Standlee (eds.), *Advancing the Cause of Liberty: Irish Women's Writing, 1878–1922* (Manchester, Manchester University Press, 2016), pp. 33–48.

———. 'Women and Fiction, 1845–1900.' In Heather Ingman and Clíona Ó Gallchoir (eds.) *A History of Modern Irish Women's Literature* (Cambridge, Cambridge University Press, 2018). pp. 96–113.

———. 'Shame is the Spur: Novels by Irish Catholics, 1873–1922.' In Liam Harte (ed.) *The Oxford Handbook of Modern Irish Fiction* (Oxford, Oxford University Press, 2020), pp. 83–98.

———. 'Rosa Mulholland.' *Cambridge Dictionary of Irish Biography.* dib-cambridge-org

O'Neill, George. 'The Poetry of Rosa Mulholland, Lady Gilbert.' *Irish Monthly* 49:580 (1921), pp. 397–405.

O'Toole, Tina. *The Irish New Woman* (Basingstoke, Palgrave Macmillan, 2013).

Declan O'Keefe, 'A Man for Others and a Beacon in the Twilight: Matthew Russell, SJ, and the *Irish Monthly*,' *Studies* 99.394 (2010), pp. 169–79.

Peterson, Linda H., *Becoming a Woman of Letters: Myths of Authorship and Facts of the Victorian Market* (Princeton, NJ, Princeton University Press, 2009).

Russell, Matthew. 'Silver Jubilee Retrospect'. *Irish Monthly* 25:283 (1897), pp. 1–6.

———. 'Poets I Have Known, VI, Rosa Mulholland.' *Donahoe's Magazine* 48:1 (1902), pp. 25–47.

Standlee, Whitney. *Power to Observe: Irish Women Novelists in Britain, 1890–1916* (Bern, Peter Lang, 2015).

Tynan, Katharine. 'Lord Russell of Killowen, Lord Chief Justice of England,' pp. 47–58; 'John and Ellen O'Leary', pp. 91–109; 'Father Matthew Russell, SJ, a Priest Editor,' pp. 145–60; 'Rosa Mulholland (Lady Gilbert), 1920,' pp. 305–22. In *Memories* (London, E. Nash and Grayson, 1924).

Ward, Mary Augusta (Mrs Humphrey). *Marcella*. London, Smith, Elder; Leipzig, Bernard Tauchnitz, 1894.

———. *Sir George Tressady* (London, Smith, Elder, 1896).

Yeats, W.B. *Representative Irish Tales* (New York, G.P. Putnam's Sons, 1891).

Also published by *EER*
Now available or coming soon

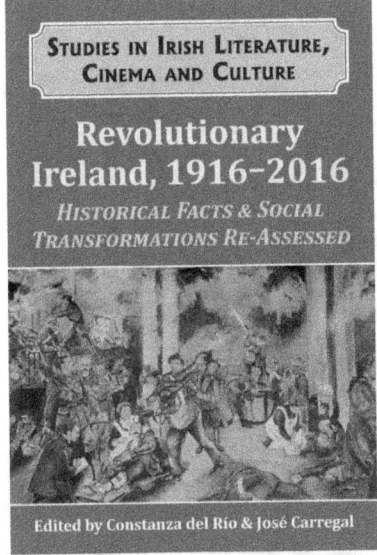

www.ingramcontent.com/pod-product-compliance
Lightning Source LLC
Chambersburg PA
CBHW052047300426
44117CB00012B/2009